CASTLES
of
ENGLAND SCOTLAND AND WALES
A GUIDE AND GAZETTEER

CASTLES

of

ENGLAND SCOTLAND AND WALES
A GUIDE AND GAZETTEER

NATHANIEL HARRIS

CHANCELLOR
PRESS

728·81

First published in 1991 by George Philip Limited
59 Grosvenor Street, London W1X 9DA

This edition published 2003 by Chancellor Press,
an imprint of Bounty Books, a division of
Octopus Publishing Group Ltd,
2-4 Heron Quays, London E14 4JP

Text © Nathaniel Harris 1991
Artwork © George Philip Limited 1991

British Library Cataloguing in Publication Data

Harris, Nathaniel
    Castles of England, Scotland and Wales.
    1. Great Britain. Castles. Visitors' guides
    I. Title
    914.104859

ISBN 0-7537-0753-5

Page design Janette Widdows
Typeset by BAS Printers Limited,
Over Wallop, Hampshire, Great Britain
Printed in Hong Kong

———◆———

Title-page illustration *Clifford's Tower in York, viewed from the north-west*

Contents

Introduction

◆

Nowadays Britain's castles are widely acknowledged to be a vital part of the national heritage. Almost all are superbly maintained by institutions or private owners, and in recent years they have attracted more visitors than ever as settings for historical re-enactments such as mock-medieval banquets and battles. But it is still not easy for visitors to identify the distinctive features of a particular castle, to locate it imaginatively in time, or to grasp why castles in general differ from one another so strikingly in size, appearance and layout.

This book offers straightforward help by explaining the development of the castle in Britain, and by describing some of the most beautiful, historic or formidable examples.

The book is organized in the following way:

Origins A brief 16-part history of British castles, chronicling developments in the arts of attack and defence, and indicating the social changes that set up conflicts between the castle's multiple functions as fortress, home and status symbol.

Gazetteer An alphabetical list of 100 selected castles to visit throughout England, Scotland and Wales. All those chosen have plenty to see above ground, ranging from spectacular ruins to still-occupied stately homes.

Maps Each of the castles described in the gazetteer is marked in red on one or more of the four preceding regional maps. In addition, six of the most splendid and historic castles in the gazetteer have been specially selected as 'Guided Tours', receiving slightly more extended treatment; these six castles are denoted on the maps by red capital letters.

Glossary A concise definition and explanation of technical terms.

Left *The ruinous interior of Hermitage Castle in Scotland*

◆

I
Origins

Of all Britain's historic strongholds and fortified places, her castles are the most substantial and stirring; but they are far from being the oldest. From the 1st century BC, the inhabitants of the far north and west of Scotland were putting up hundreds of round drystone towers, or *brochs*, to protect their settlements. Further south, the Celtic population of what are now England and Wales created vast hillforts by digging ditches and throwing up ramparts to create complex defensive systems. These, however, proved no match for the Roman legions who began their conquest of Britain in AD 43, bringing with them a range of new military techniques and creating a city-based culture and a network of straight, well-made roads.

The inhabitants of Romano-British cities were protected by town walls; the troops, being professionals, were maintained as the garrisons of forts laid out with the geometric precision so characteristic of Roman planning, or were deployed along the great walls built in the north to keep out the Picts and Scots. Roman rule lasted until about AD 405, when the legions were recalled in an effort to cope with the deepening crisis closer to home. Waves of barbarian peoples overran most of the Roman world, including the Romanized province of Britain. After a bitter struggle lasting some 200 years, England was occupied by a group of Germanic peoples, the Anglo-Saxons, who absorbed most of the surviving Celtic inhabitants; but in Wales, Scotland and Ireland the Celts retained their independence and distinctive identity. Over the next few centuries, Anglo-Saxon England became Christian and was forged into a single kingdom as a response to new invasions by Vikings from Scandinavia who were ultimately defeated and integrated into Saxon society. In the process, the Anglo-Saxons developed their own national system of defence, based on an army combining élite troops (house-carls) with militiamen (the fyrd), while in theory the existence of fortified towns, or *burhs* ('boroughs'), impeded the progress of any invader.

In practice the burhs offered little effective resistance to William the Conqueror, once the Norman duke had defeated King Harold's army at the Battle of Hastings in 1066. The Norman Conquest ushered in a new era, one in which the principal battle-winner was the armoured man on horseback, or knight, and the typical

Left The Roman outer walls on the west side of Pevensey Castle

9

fortification was the castle. Earlier defence works, whether garrisoned forts or burhs, had been directly or indirectly designed to protect the community; but the medieval castle was essentially a private stronghold, built to protect – and also to glorify – its lord. As such it was the product of the feudal system, in which nobles all over the land played a self-supporting military role in the organization and control of society, and consequently enjoyed a high degree of independence; even royal castles were in a sense private, for the feudal monarch saw himself in many respects as a great landowner, travelling from one of his estates to the next, living off its produce, and finding security and comfort in one of his castles nearby.

The comfort, if rudimentary by modern standards, was another distinguishing feature of the castle. It was not simply a barracks to house soldiers, or an otherwise uninviting refuge in emergencies, although these might on some occasions be among its functions. It was also a residence in which the lord and his family could live in splendour during peaceful times, and maintain a reasonable state even during a siege. Monarchs and great nobles, of course, possessed many castles and could not be permanently in residence at more than one, but in such cases a substitute resident – a person of some consequence, named as constable or castellan – was put in charge.

Private stronghold and personal residence: these are the essential characteristics of the medieval castle, although inevitably no single definition will cover every fortress that common speech and common sense are content to label a castle. Almost from the beginning there was some conflict between the need for security and the desire for comfort; for example, if there is to be enough light for pleasurable living on the ground floor, windows must be larger and consequently more vulnerable to penetration by an enemy. Such problems could initially be solved by compromise or ingenuity, but grew more acute as standards of convenience and luxury became higher. By the late Middle Ages, many castles were being built with such a mixture of defensive artfulness and apparent disregard for obvious but uncomfortable precautions that historians have found it difficult to judge just how seriously they were intended to withstand an attacker.

Such questions became meaningful because, at an early date, castles acquired a range of non-defensive functions: as repositories of records and administrative centres, as prisons, and above all as symbols of lordship. Unchallenged except by the great edifices of Mother Church, they dominated the landscape, proclaiming the quasi-divine nature of secular authority. In time, although social and military changes made them less and less useful as fortresses, the potency of castles as symbols ensured their survival in one form or another. Towards the end of the Middle Ages they seem often to have been built as a proclamation of status, especially by those who had just acquired or enhanced it; and although no true castles were put up after the 16th century, their image remained powerful enough

A CONSTABLE'S SEAL

SOME EARLY BRITISH FORTIFICATIONS
The best-preserved and most accessible brochs are Mousa on Shetland and Dun Carloway on Lewis. Maiden Castle is a huge, impressive hillfort in Dorset. Roman fortifications include Hadrian's Wall (running from the Solway to the Tyne) and forts such as Reculver and Richborough (both in Kent). The earthworks and wooden palisades of the burhs have vanished, but Offa's Dyke, the great defensive ditch separating England and Wales, survives as an example of Anglo-Saxon energy.

to encourage the use of battlements, turrets and other pseudo-martial features on palaces and mansions, and soon afterwards to prompt the building of a sham castle such as at BOLSOVER (Derbyshire).

Thereafter the castle enjoyed a long posthumous history. Imitations of variable accuracy were built, right down to the 20th century, in a spirit of antiquarian romanticism, Gothic fantasy or sheer megalomania; peaceful but palatial mansions continued to be called 'castles', and the battlemented suburban villa and turreted public house testified to the hold of the medieval originals on the popular imagination. Beginning in stern reality, the castle has ended in the realm of myth; and although this book is mainly concerned with 'true' castles, both sides of their long history have received some attention.

THE CONQUERORS AND THEIR CASTLES

Almost the first action taken by Duke William after landing on the Sussex coast was to put up a castle at PEVENSEY (East Sussex). With a typical Norman sense of economy he sited it within Anderida, a large Roman fort whose stone walls offered ready-made protection against attack. The work was evidently carried out very swiftly, for William landed on 28 September 1066 and had moved on by 14 October, when he commanded at the battle on Senlac Hill near Hastings in which his men fought and overcame King Harold's Saxon army. It has been plausibly suggested that this first, speedy example of castle-building was executed with prefabricated timber parts, brought over by the Norman fleet.

Following his victory, William built a castle at Hastings, refortified DOVER (Kent), and, once London had submitted, began a castle there to ensure the continued obedience of the capital. Within a few years William had campaigned over much of England and had planted castles beside or within all the main Saxon towns; meanwhile, his followers were taking control of the estates they had received from the new king, and were putting up their own strongholds.

All this makes it clear that the Normans attached great importance to castles in their invasion, conquest and settlement of England. One reason was that the castle served an impressive variety of purposes. It was a refuge in times of danger or defeat, and it provided the new alien lords with security from riot and surprise. But there were also more positive military advantages. The castle was a highly visible strongpoint, effective in overawing a hostile population; and it could be used as a forward base during a general advance, securing freshly gained territory against risings and counter-attacks. This last function came to the fore in the 1090s, when the Normans advanced into South Wales, and would be the key to the final conquest of the principality two centuries later. The wider defensive

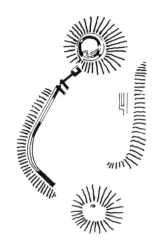

EARTHWORKS OF LEWES CASTLE

Left *The Norman keep at Portchester Castle, with the Roman walls beyond*

virtues of a network of castles were summarized by a second-generation Anglo-Norman writer, Ordericus Vitalis, who blamed their absence directly for the feebleness of English resistance after the Battle of Hastings.

During the reign of William the Conqueror (1066–87) hundreds of castles were built in England, differing from one another not only in size and materials, but also in design. This probably reflected the newness of castles – even in France they were only some 50 years old by 1066 – and also the character of William's 'Norman' following, which actually included many Bretons and other French volunteers, each with a slightly different military experience and approach to fortification.

In many instances it was simply the lie of the land that determined a castle's plan. At RICHMOND (North Yorkshire), for example, the Breton Alan the Red chose to build on a high triangular platform with a sheer cliff face on one side; to make it defensible he had only to put up walls on the two more vulnerable edges, placing a strong gatehouse at the junction. However, such naturally advantageous sites are relatively rare in England, and a more common Norman practice was to take over an artificial site – one at which some form of fortification survived from a past age. A Roman fort could be converted into a castle by digging a ditch across one corner and erecting a tower or hall inside it; the larger area beyond the ditch became a useful enclosure, or *bailey*, and the Roman walls provided instant, free and very efficient protection for the inmates. This was done at PEVENSEY, CARDIFF (South Glamorgan) and, somewhat later, PORTCHESTER (Hampshire). Roman or earlier earthworks could also be adapted to 11th-century requirements, as at DOVER (Kent) and CARISBROOKE (Isle of Wight).

Earthworks are a very ancient method of fortification, generally constructed by digging a deep ditch round a camp or settlement and heaping up the earth that has been removed in the process so that it forms a rampart on the inner side of the ditch; when a palisade or wall is put up along the top of the rampart, any attacker is faced with a daunting, dangerous, tiring climb from the bottom of the ditch before he can even engage the enemy. (The water-filled moat is a relatively late development, usually requiring sophisticated channelling operations.) Many post-Conquest castles were *ringworks* of this sort, protecting the lord's hall and possibly other buildings; a larger ditch-demarcated enclosure (the bailey) held stables and other functions.

Ringworks, like all but a handful of 11th-century castles, were built of timber, which was quicker, easier and cheaper to use than stone. These were considerations of special importance in the post-Conquest situation, when security was a matter of some urgency.

In the later years of the century, the timber *motte-and-bailey* castle won a wide popularity that it retained for almost a hundred years. Its characteristic feature was the *motte*, a tall, cone-shaped, flat-topped mound on which stood the lord's tower, surrounded by a palisade. A ditch ran round the base of the motte, and also round the bailey below and adjoining it, giving the layout a rough figure-eight outline. Motte and bailey were linked by a flying bridge which could be removed if the bailey was overrun by an attacking force.

The motte was usually, though not invariably, an artificial mound, giving a castle the height denied it by the terrain. The advantages of height – of making the besieger toil upwards while missiles rained down on him – were obvious; but the symbolic and psychological aspects of loftiness also helped to make the motte-and-bailey castle an almost automatic choice. The timber of these castles has long since rotted in the British climate, but many abandoned mottes have been uncovered by archaeologists. Others survive, but have been subsequently built on; and in fact the later development of such famous castles as WINDSOR (Berkshire), ARUNDEL (West Sussex), CARISBROOKE and CAERNARFON (Gwynedd) can be said to have been determined by their motte-and-bailey origin.

CASTLES OF STONE

While they remained in use, most castles were subject to frequent, more or less drastic alterations prompted by military developments or seigneurial fashion. Obsolete or outmoded features were swept away or overlaid – a process visible even within a few years of the Conquest, at sites where, for example, an early ringwork might be 'improved' by the addition of a motte. But the biggest single change during the Norman period was the very gradual increase in the number of stone castles, which ultimately became indispensable possessions for any lord who aspired to independence and prestige.

The advantages of building in stone were obvious: it was more durable and resistant than timber, and above all it was less vulnerable to assault by fire. The drawbacks were that it cost much more and took much longer, both weighty considerations at a time when Norman lords were settling in on their new estates. Building in stone also required very sophisticated skills by comparison with the digging and joinery that sufficed to create motte-and-bailey castles, which must in most cases have been put up by more or less forced local labour. For all these reasons the transition to stone was very gradual, and the timber motte-and-bailey castle remained extremely common until the second half of the 12th century.

Nevertheless, a few stone castles began to be built in England as early as the 1070s, and two were royal foundations, quite exceptional in size and appearance. The White Tower, guarding and/or intimidating London, replaced William's first castle outside the city; and COLCHESTER CASTLE (Essex) was raised on the foundations of a Roman temple. (The White Tower is now the nucleus of the extensive

OTHER POST-CONQUEST CASTLES

Among the castles put up by or for William the Conqueror to overawe Saxon towns, Exeter (Devon) was built of stone, and consequently some remains survive. It is also an example of a ringwork, built within the Roman town walls. The mottes of William's castles survive at Lincoln and York. Lydford (Devon) nestles in a British hillfort, and so does the huge motte of Thetford (Norfolk) and the ringwork of Old Sarum (Wiltshire).

Restormel Castle, a classic example of the English shell keep

castle rather misleadingly called the TOWER OF LONDON.) These massive rectangular edifices were examples of the *keep*, a type of stone building that housed a hall, chapel, kitchens and everything else needed to make its occupants safe and self-sufficient behind its extremely thick walls, enabling it to withstand a siege on its own, even if the enemy overran all the outer defences.

One of King William's most trusted lieutenants, William Fitz Osbern, put up a keep for himself at CHEPSTOW (Gwent) soon after the Conquest. But other royal subjects who managed to build in stone at this early date chose a simpler, cheaper arrangement. At ROCHESTER (Kent), RICHMOND (North Yorkshire) and LUDLOW (Shropshire) they protected their halls and other residential buildings by surrounding them with a strong, high wall. This kind of non-load-bearing wall, known as a *curtain wall*, was reinforced at intervals along its length by towers, and a strongly defended gateway in the wall gave access to the interior.

Although the curtain-wall castle would eventually come into its own, for a long time to come the preferred model for those who could afford it was the keep. Significantly, in the course of the 12th century the gatehouses at RICHMOND and LUDLOW were converted into keeps, and in the 1130s the curtain-wall castle at ROCHESTER was dwarfed by the addition of the high, splendid keep which is now its chief ornament.

KEEP AT CARDIFF CASTLE

Keeps are often classified into two types: the *hall keep*, oblong and generally two storeys high, and the more obviously vertical, three- or four-storey *tower keep*. CHEPSTOW, COLCHESTER and the White Tower may be considered hall keeps, and the type appeared in the early 12th century at NORWICH and CASTLE RISING (both in Norfolk). But following the example of CORFE (Dorset) at the beginning of the 12th century, tower keeps were built at ROCHESTER and HEDINGHAM CASTLE (Essex), and by the late 12th century this had become the standard type, its extra height offering both military and psychological advantages.

The design of the keep allowed the defenders only a limited activity: its supreme asset was the sheer thickness of the walls. For this reason, accessible points of entry were denied the attackers. Apertures at ground-floor level were restricted to tiny windows and arrow-slits; the dim-lit interior was used mainly as a storage area, and gracious, well-lit living began on the first floor in the hall. For the same reason, the entrance to the keep was at first-floor level, reached by means of a flight of external steps. From the 12th century the steps were encased in a *forebuilding*, built flush against the main structure, which made the prospect of fighting his way in even more hazardous for the besieger, while incidentally providing extra space for a chapel or some similar amenity. A keep was usually generously *battered* (its walls reinforced so that they inclined outwards towards their base) to withstand ramming or undermining. By contrast, the *pilaster strips* (flat buttress-like vertical strips running down the outside of most keeps) were decorative rather than functional, except perhaps where they encased and supported

ARROW-SLIT

the corners. As symbols of lordship, keeps were objects of display; and as the name of the White Tower reminds us, they were commonly whitewashed and, given their height, must have been conspicuous for many miles.

Keeps were not built to replace the timber towers of motte-and-bailey castles, if only because an artificial mound could not have been relied on to bear such a mass of stone. In any case, the keep was really a separate development, offering an alternative way of obtaining the lofty height attained by such towers. Generally speaking, lords of motte-and-bailey castles who wanted to make the transition to stone either abandoned the old site or adapted it. The simplest way to adapt was to replace the palisade on the top of the motte with a stone wall; this, known as a *shell keep*, became the principal defence, the tower within usually being replaced by a range of residential buildings. The classic English shell keep is RESTORMEL (Cornwall), but other fine examples include LEWES (East Sussex), ARUNDEL (West Sussex), CARISBROOKE (Isle of Wight), WINDSOR (Berkshire), TAMWORTH (Staffordshire) and CARDIFF (South Glamorgan). LAUNCESTON (Cornwall) is a rare example of a shell keep enclosing a (later) stone tower. A very different method of construction was employed at FARNHAM (Surrey) and BERKELEY (Gloucestershire), where the stone shell was built up from the base of the motte, encasing it. The dating of shell keeps is imprecise, but their vogue seems to have been largely confined to the 12th century.

<hr/>

FEUDAL LORDSHIP

Feudalism was the dominant social system in Europe for most of the Middle Ages, and the castle was one of its characteristic institutions. Consequently, some knowledge of the workings of feudal society is helpful in understanding the part – or parts – played by the castle within it. What follows is, of course, a schematic 'ideal' version of a more complex and mutable phenomenon.

One way of viewing feudalism is as a pyramid or hierarchy of landlords and tenants, its distinctive feature being that the 'rent' at most levels was military rather than financial. At the apex of the social pyramid was the monarch, who was almost always male. As the 'owner' of the realm, he made large land grants to his principal followers, who were actually known as *tenants-in-chief*. The lands he retained – his demesne – served to support him; what he required from the tenants-in-chief in return for their great holdings, or *honours*, was an undertaking to do military service under his command for a fixed number of days in every year, and to bring with them a stipulated number of fully equipped knights-at-arms.

So the feudal system was, among other things, a way of trying to ensure that

OTHER EARLY STONE CASTLES
Castle Acre (Norfolk) is a keep that actually originated as a hall within a ringwork; it was fortified *c.* 1100. At Guildford (Surrey) the castle keep was built right next to the abandoned motte. Shell keeps include Totnes (Devon) and Berkhamsted (Hertfordshire). Curtain-wall castles were erected at Peveril (Derbyshire) and Brough (Cumbria) before 1100, although only short lengths of 11th-century wall survive.

The interior of the great hall at Hedingham Castle

adequate forces were always available to the Crown in a relatively poor and decentralized society which could not support a standing army. In order to fulfil their obligations to the king, the tenants-in-chief granted lands to a number of baronial followers who held these *fiefs* in return for attendance and knight service; and the pattern was repeated at a variable number of levels down to the individual knight. He, along with his armour, weapons and horse (the accoutrements that made him the most formidable fighting machine of the age), was maintained by the fief he held from his immediate lord – or rather it was the serfs at the base of the pyramid, working the land and being obliged to sacrifice part of their produce and labour, who supported the knight and all the other members of the hierarchy.

The feudal contract was given another dimension by the ceremonial that bound lord and vassal together in a personal relationship. Both took solemn oaths, and the vassal put his hands between his lord's, swearing fealty and doing homage – that is, vowing to be faithful and acknowledging that he was the lord's 'man'. The obligations were mutual, for the lord formally extended his protection to the vassal, and the two were committed to stand by each other in (almost) all circumstances. If they fell out, the lord could summon his erring vassal for judgement in his court, while the vassal who believed himself wronged could issue a 'defiance', breaking the tie in due form – and, probably, preparing to defend himself.

A prime result of the feudal system was to distribute authority widely rather than concentrate it at the centre, although the balance would shift in one direction or another in the course of the Middle Ages. At each level the lord-vassal relationship was the norm, and its institutions – including the castle – would be replicated. The tenant-in-chief would live in near-royal style in his castle, with a large household of retainers and servants, and exercise near-royal powers on his estates, administering them and giving justice to his vassals and serfs; and his conduct would be imitated, as far as they were able, by his vassals and his vassals' vassals.

Something of the sort was probably inevitable, since the medieval king had neither the resources nor the means of communication with which to exercise close control over more than a limited area of his realm. But the potential threat posed by 'over-mighty subjects' was apparent, and monarchs did what they could to ensure that the magnates could not consolidate their estates into large blocs of territory. In England, William I took advantage of the fact that he had conquered the country at a stroke, distributing over a wide area the estates with which he rewarded his followers. The main exceptions were the lords stationed on the border lands, or *Marches*, close to Wales and Scotland, whose exceptional power and independence reflected their hazardous 'front-line' situation; and in the event, the Marcher lords in the west and the Bishop of Durham – master of the large Palatinate of Durham created as a bulwark against the Scots – proved to be among

SEAL OF WILLIAM I

the most troublesome subjects of successive Norman kings.

As this indicates, feudal allegiances were easily strained. Although lordship and loyalty were at the heart of the chivalric code, ambition, pride, interest or a taste for intrigue often overrode them. A strong king might provoke a serious rebellion; the reign of a weak or unlucky one might be even more disastrous, since the decay of royal authority allowed the outbreak of private wars between lords great and small. In such a situation the castle ceased to be a centre and symbol of lordship, reverting to the fortress function for which its massively thick walls were built.

The scattered nature of their estates encouraged the king and his tenants-in-chief to build numerous castles. Many lesser lords must have possessed a single manor and just one hall or castle; but great ones needed many residences, since they moved about constantly. In a small-scale society where relationships were based on personal rather than institutional contacts, it was important for a lord to show himself and make his presence felt by all those whose loyalty or obedience he claimed. And there was also a simple economic reason for this peripatetic way of life: the lord and his retinue of dependants and servants lived off his estates, and therefore travelled round them from one source of vittles – orchards, fish-ponds, well-filled barns and good hunting for fresh meat – to the next. Not every such place was a castle, but it was certainly useful to know that there was one not too far away, available for ceremonial demonstrations of authority, the banking of treasure or refuge in an emergency.

———◆———

ANARCHY AND ORDER: THE 12TH CENTURY

An important factor in a king's struggle to keep his barons in order was his ability to control their castle-building activities. In England, no castle could be put up without royal consent, granted in the form of a licence to crenellate (that is, to build a battlemented structure). In the early Norman period such licences were normally issued to trusted followers or relations, although there was of course no way of guaranteeing that they or their descendants would remain loyal to the Crown. And the withholding of a licence, like other royal prerogatives, had substance only if it could be enforced.

On the whole, 'good order' – very much a medieval ideal – was maintained under the first three Norman kings: William I (1066–87), William II 'Rufus' (1087–1100) and Henry I (1100–35). Each was a strong personality in his own way, and capable of ruthless action against turbulent subjects; while at the same time, the wisdom of maintaining a show of solidarity in a newly conquered land may also have encouraged baronial restraint.

Left *Conisbrough Castle began its transition to stone in the 1180s*

Typically, a major breakdown of authority occurred when the succession to the throne was disputed. Lacking a direct male heir after his son had drowned, Henry I tried to ensure the succession of his daughter Matilda by forcing the barons to swear fealty to her during his own lifetime. But on Henry's death, his nephew Stephen of Blois persuaded most of the baronage to support him. The Crown was weakened by the concessions he was forced to make, and when Matilda landed to assert her claim, a civil war ensued that was destructive in itself as well as enabling the barons to benefit from the competition of the two sides for their allegiance. The 19 years of Stephen's reign (1135–54) came to be known as 'the Anarchy', letting loose civil war, private wars between feuding barons, and a lordly crime wave with no higher objective than loot. According to the *Peterborough Chronicle*:

> *They were all forsworn and their oaths broken. For every great man built himself castles and held them against the King; and they filled the entire land with these castles. They sorely burdened the unhappy people of the country with forced labour on the castles; and when they were built they filled them with devils and wicked men.*

The chronicler describes torture, the extortion of protection money and the plundering of the countryside as commonplace, so that 'men said openly that Christ and His saints slept'.

Although medieval chroniclers were prone to paint their scenes in strong colours, this is an impressive indictment. The huge number of castles built during the Anarchy were almost all adulterine (unlicensed), put up in defiance of an impotent royal authority, and most of them must have been rapidly constructed timber works on mottes. Sieges abounded – some are glanced at on pages 24 and 29 – and the many thrilling episodes included the capture of King Stephen and Matilda's flight in the snow from her besieged castle at Oxford. But no definite result ensued.

The war ended at last with an agreement that Stephen should reign until his death, when Matilda's son Henry would succeed him. Henry II (1154–89), England's first Angevin king, became one of the most powerful rulers in Europe, acquiring more than half of France by inheritance and marriage. Vigorous and strong-minded, he restored and extended royal authority in England, in the process dismantling great numbers of adulterine castles – as many as a thousand according to some estimates.

Henry was also a great builder of castles, erecting a series of increasingly splendid and sophisticated keeps whose interiors were designed for a high degree of royal comfort. Most of them, whether inland (KENILWORTH, Warwickshire) or part of a chain of coastal defences (BAMBURGH, Northumberland; SCARBOROUGH, North Yorkshire; DOVER, Kent), followed the accepted rectangular plan, as did

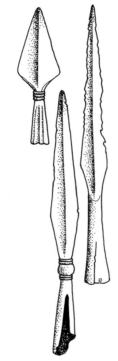

NORMAN SPEARHEADS

such ecclesiastical or noble keeps as NORHAM (Northumberland), MIDDLEHAM (North Yorkshire) and APPLEBY (Cumbria).

But there were also experiments with new plans, since it had become increasingly clear that the rectangular keep had serious military drawbacks. In particular, its pronounced corners were vulnerable to bombardment, and when sappers undermined a corner – digging away the earth beneath it – the resulting collapse was more calamitous than in the case of a straight or curved surface. At ORFORD (Suffolk) Henry II tried to solve the problem by building a polygonal keep whose 21 sides made it virtually round; and shortly afterwards Henry's half-brother built an entirely round tower at CONISBROUGH (South Yorkshire). Both, however, added long, large buttresses or turrets on the outside – no less than six at CONISBROUGH – that probably nullified any benefits offered by the new designs. Henry himself cannot have been entirely convinced, for he went on to spend enormous sums on DOVER CASTLE, which can be regarded as the supreme English rectangular keep.

This kind of keep retained certain advantages: it was easier to build than a round keep, and it was a far more convenient shape when it came to dividing the space available into rooms. So it may not have been conservatism alone that led to the building of a rectangular keep such as HELMSLEY (North Yorkshire) even after DOVER, and to the perpetuation of this tradition by lesser lords for at least another century.

The advantages of the round keep were most clearly realized in South Wales, where Norman and Welsh lords were locked in combat and it was a matter of some urgency to apply the latest and best in military thinking. The new design was used by both sides, most majestically *c.* 1200 at PEMBROKE CASTLE (Dyfed), built by the leading knight of the age, William Marshal. Even at that date, however, the seeds had been sown of still more radical changes that would bring the curtain-wall castle back into favour.

—◆—

ATTACKING A CASTLE

Since 'human error' is a universal phenomenon, the most effective and least costly way of capturing a castle was by speed, surprise or trickery. Given the resources poured into castle-building, it is astonishing quite how often attackers managed to take a fortress by rushing an open gateway, smuggling themselves in disguised as laundrywomen, or passing themselves off as friends by giving the defenders' battle-cry! One of the most strongly defended places in Europe, Richard the Lionheart's Château Gaillard, was captured by a handful of soldiers who climbed into the castle through the latrine shaft and put the garrison to

OTHER 12TH-CENTURY KEEPS
Henry II built rectangular keeps at Carlisle (Cumbria) and, on a smaller scale, Newcastle-upon-Tyne (Tyne and Wear). Goodrich (Hereford and Worcester) and Brougham (Cumbria) were also rectangular, as were such Welsh examples as Ogmore and Coity (both in Mid Glamorgan) and Dolwyddelan (Gwynedd), which represented an efficient native adaptation of the Norman type. Chilham (Kent) boasts an octagonal keep. Among late 12th-century and early 13th-century round keeps in Wales were Bronllys (Powys), Dolbadarn (Gwynedd) and Skenfrith (Gwent).

flight, presumably with a combination of shock tactics and intolerable pungency.

When resources of this kind were not available, and negotiations, threats and bluff had failed to achieve anything, the besiegers had three options: they could try to reduce the castle by blockade, by an immediate assault, or by weakening the defences as a preliminary to a final assault.

A blockade, intended to starve out the defending garrison, was economical of lives but costly in time and resources. The besieging army was immobilized for the duration, and since most vassals' attendance on their lords – including the king – was limited to 40 days, there was a real possibility that the feudal host might simply melt away. The occupants of a carefully provisioned castle with a reliable well could hope to outlast most besiegers including the king, since there was a good chance that his difficulties would encourage disaffection elsewhere, making it hard for him to carry a single siege through to the end – a situation in which the unlucky Stephen found himself several times. However, long sieges were by no means unknown, and when Baldwin de Redvers, a typical baronial ruffian, took advantage of conditions during the Anarchy to seize the royal castle at Exeter in Devon, he held out against Stephen for three months and could have gone on even longer if Exeter's two wells had not inexplicably failed, parching the garrison into submission when they had used up their supplies of wine for drinking, washing and cooking.

If a siege was likely to be a protracted affair, the attackers settled into any nearby buildings that could be fortified, or even built a siege castle of their own from which to conduct operations. The outline of such a 'counter-castle' is visible close to Huntingdon Castle in Cambridgeshire, and William II is recorded as having erected one right up against BAMBURGH CASTLE (Northumberland); it was evidently effective enough for the BAMBURGH garrison to nickname it *malvoisin* ('bad neighbour'). However, BAMBURGH did not surrender until its lord, Robert de Mowbray, was captured outside the castle and paraded in chains before his wife with the threat that his eyes would be put out unless she opened the gates.

A direct attack with fire and the sword had a fair chance of success against a timber castle; but a stone castle was another matter. While its walls remained intact, the attackers' main hope lay in *escalade* – climbing up ladders placed against the walls and fighting their way over the parapet. This was risky, although it might succeed if it could be mounted simultaneously at many points, and with intense covering fire that made the defenders duck and prevented them from pushing the ladders away or cutting down each man as he reached the top. In 1140 one of the bad barons of the Anarchy, Robert Fitz Hubert, brought off a surprise escalade at night, leaving the army of Matilda, with which he was supposed to be serving, riding to Devizes in Wiltshire and sending his men up leather ladders into the unsuspecting royal castle – which he thereupon declared that he held for neither Stephen nor Matilda, but for himself!

Bamburgh Castle occupies a superb defensive site on a rocky headland

An alternative method of storming the battlements was to build a belfry or siege tower. This was a tall wooden structure, boarded in to protect the occupants, which was wheeled up to the castle wall; then a drawbridge was dropped from the belfry on to the parapet, and fighting men poured across it into the castle. For such a contraption to reach the castle wall, the ditch around it had to be packed solid with earth or stones in order to bear its weight (an operation carried out under enemy fire); and although the belfry would be hung with wet hides, there was every chance that the enemy would manage to set it on fire, with disastrous consequences.

The bottom storey of the belfry could also be used as cover for men wielding a battering ram or picks in an attempt to make a breach in the wall. More commonly, such operations were carried out separately, beneath a kind of low shed called a *cat* or *penthouse*, which was somewhat less vulnerable than the belfry.

The defenders found it much harder to do anything about underground tunnelling, designed to undermine and bring down a section of the castle wall. The diggings were supported by timbers until they were complete; then these props were set on fire, the sappers made their exit, and the now unsupported wall collapsed into the tunnel. The vulnerability of corners was shown at ROCHESTER (Kent) in 1215, when King John's men brought down the south-east angle of the keep; combustion was provided by animal fat, the King sending for 'forty of the fattest pigs of the sort least good for eating to bring fire beneath the tower'.

In the 12th century, powerful missile-throwing machines came back into use; although known in antiquity, they had long been neglected and probably owed their revival to westerners' experiences during the Crusades. The main types were the *ballista*, a giant crossbow that could skewer several men with one shot, and the *mangonel*, a spoon-shaped catapult worked by torsion (twisting a rope to pull back the arm, and then abruptly releasing it). In the 13th century a genuine medieval invention was introduced: the *trébuchet*, a sling worked by counterweights, on the principle of the see-saw. King John's missiles, unlike his mines, failed to make a breach at ROCHESTER, and it seems that these apparently formidable weapons were never very effective against really strong castles. The basic principle of the castle – the impregnability of massively thick walls – would retain its essential validity throughout the Middle Ages.

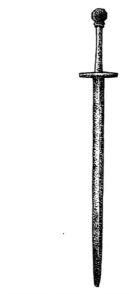

TWO-HANDED MEDIEVAL SWORD

BALLISTA

Right Rochester Castle was besieged in 1215 by King John

THE DEFENDERS' RESOURCES

Once the bailey of a castle was overrun, the defenders were forced to rely for their salvation on the thickness of the keep walls. During the 12th century the danger of escalade was reduced by a general heightening of walls, and the

most vulnerable point – the entrance – was strengthened by the introduction of the forebuilding and the gradual adoption of the *portcullis*. This was an immensely heavy timber grid culminating in a row of iron-capped points along its bottom. It was raised by a windlass in a room above the gateway or passage that it blocked, running within grooves cut in the stone walls at the side. Its great advantages were that it could be lowered instantly in an emergency by simply letting the windlass turn freely, and that it was effectively impossible to stop its downward progress; moreover, once down, it could not be thrust or levered open, but had to be destroyed before the attacker could make further progress.

Nevertheless, it remained important to hinder enemy activity outside the walls, slowing down operations such as ramming and mining. The best and safest place to do this from was the battlements, of which the outer edge was a parapet. Along its top ran the familiar up-down-up-down line of rectangular solids and voids; the solids, known as *merlons*, offered the garrison cover while they fired or flung missiles down on the enemy through the voids, or *crenels*. (Crenels were generally covered by wooden shutters hinged at the top, but these have long since vanished.) This arrangement – crenellation – became a kind of symbolic short-hand for the castle, and royal permission to build a fortified private dwelling was embodied in a licence to crenellate. Behind this parapet lay the wall-walk or sentry-walk, which was fenced off behind by another parapet (technically known as the *parados*).

CRENELLATION

It was difficult for the defenders to operate effectively against the vital area immediately adjacent to the base of a keep, although the substitution of round for rectangular designs removed 'blind' corners as well as strengthening the walls. One solution was to build projecting towers or turrets on to the keep. Another – far more economical – was to erect temporary wooden hoardings on beams projecting from the wall head; at a number of castles the visitor can identify the holes in the masonry into which such beams were fixed. The sort of missiles flung down on the besiegers would probably have been rocks, burning tow to fire protective devices such as the cat, or, at a pinch, scalding hot water; the story-book favourite, boiling oil, seems a most expensive and unlikely option. A second-ary advantage of the battering at the base of the wall was that its inclined surface improved the garrison's chances of hitting the enemy by devastating, unpredictable ricochets.

At other levels, archers could fire at the enemy through slits, or loops, that were very narrow on the exterior but splayed out inside to an *embrasure* – an arched area cut in the wall, with a ledge on which the archer could kneel; this allowed him to get as close as possible to the slit and position himself at various angles, thus enlarging his field of fire. The vertical arrow-slit was usually slightly wider at the bottom, enabling the archer to aim and fire down into the area at the foot of the tower. At DOVER CASTLE (Kent), Henry II's most expensive project, embrasures were equipped with no less than three arrow-slits, giving the archer a still wider field of fire. Whether he was capable of taking much advantage of it is questionable, since the bow was not a particularly powerful or accurate weapon during the early Middle Ages; significantly, many castle-builders did without arrow-slits at all, and they only became really common in the 13th century. Cruciform slits appeared at about the same time at FRAMLINGHAM (Suffolk) and DOVER, enabling the horizontally-held crossbow to be used effectively; although laborious to load, its superior accuracy made it an excellent defensive weapon.

A variety of other techniques were employed by beleaguered garrisons; and some of them seem – at least in retrospect – rather comic. Mattresses could be lowered to muffle the impact of a battering ram against a wall. During an escalade, the defenders might use long, forked poles to push away into space the ladders being climbed by an assault force. And various kinds of grapnels and pincers were manipulated to nip and pluck at cats and belfries, and also at men. While King Stephen was besieging LUDLOW CASTLE (Shropshire), the King of Scotland's son – Stephen's 'guest' or hostage – found himself caught by the seat of his breeches and swung up into the air by an iron hook thrown from a window like a fishing line. Fortunately for him, the chivalrous Stephen managed to get him down before the line was reeled in.

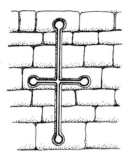

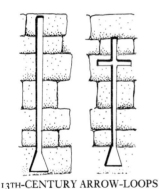

13TH-CENTURY ARROW-LOOPS

An alert garrison could sometimes see or hear evidence of mining operations close to the walls; one sensible precaution was to put out bowls of water along their length, since any underground activity would then show up in the agitations on the surface of the liquid. But when this was detected, there was not much the garrison could do unless they were willing to dig a countermine to break into the enemy tunnel, hoping to slaughter the sappers and wreck the workings before they reached their objective. One danger of such a measure was that the countermine might itself weaken the castle wall; but the risk was taken on occasion, leading to savage underground struggles. Despite the premium on secrecy, some mines must have been surprisingly high and wide, for we hear accounts of jousts being held in their galleries, sometimes even involving men on horseback.

Even a successful undermining operation need not spell the end for a really powerful keep such as at ROCHESTER (Kent). A rectangular keep usually had a cross-wall – a strong vertical wall dividing the interior from top to bottom. This doubled the number of rooms and also constituted a defensible barrier, as King John discovered at ROCHESTER after the undermining of the south-east corner; his troops rushed in and took possession, but the rebels fought on behind the cross-wall and were only forced to surrender through starvation, not sapping.

However, despite its all too solid virtues, in the 13th century the keep ceased to be regarded as the heart of the castle's defensive system.

HARLECH'S TWIN-TOWERED
GATEHOUSE

THE 13TH CENTURY

At the very time when the round keep was becoming more popular with new builders than the older rectangular form, a type of castle was being developed that was radically different from either. In this, the main defensive emphasis was shifted from holding out in the keep to manning a higher, more efficiently fortified outer curtain wall that would make it impossible for the attacker to penetrate into the area it enclosed. Keeps already stood within baileys that were enclosed by stone walls, but these were sometimes completely plain and, even when protected by mural towers, were generally expected to do no more than hold up an enemy advance towards the critical confrontation around the keep. As we have seen, LUDLOW (Shropshire) and some other castles did dispense with a keep and rely on a strong curtain; but they did not anticipate the scientific layout which made the new type of curtain-wall castle so effective.

Its distinctive feature was the placing of high, projecting towers at short, regular intervals along the curtain. This allowed the defenders in the towers to direct flanking fire along the adjacent sections of curtain when the besiegers reached it; and if the assault was concentrated at one point, the attackers could find themselves caught in a devastating crossfire from the towers on either side of them. Moreover, thanks to this arrangement, no part of the field immediately in front of the curtain was out of range, since the 'dead ground' below and in front of a tower – always difficult for a defender to aim at without exposing himself – could now be covered from the neighbouring towers. Building the towers even higher than the walls offered a further advantage, since it meant that an enemy who did succeed in reaching the wall-walk would still be subjected to a hail of missiles from above. Each of the towers was in effect a small fortress, sealed off from the bailey or courtyard below, so that the attackers might have to fight their way right round the perimeter of the castle, taking one tower after another, before all resistance was eliminated.

The new arrangement made for a much more spacious way of living. Existing keep-and-bailey castles were brought up to date by the addition of a new curtain that usually enclosed a very large outer bailey. It had already become common for lords to build additional, more comfortable residential and domestic buildings outside the keep which they could at least use in times of peace; and the possession of a strong curtain and extra space encouraged this tendency. The mural towers themselves offered more accommodation of a kind that satisfied the growing taste for privacy. New castles very often consisted of just the curtain wall and interval towers, dispensing altogether with a keep; they are sometimes called *castles of enceinte*, the enceinte being the outline (literally 'girdle') of the outermost enclosing wall.

The earliest significant examples of the curtain wall with regular interval towers occurred close to the end of the 12th century and included both adaptations and

Left *The 13th-century south curtain wall of Beeston Castle*

an entirely new castle. Henry II erected such a curtain round his great rectangular keep at DOVER (Kent), and another round the shell keep at WINDSOR (Berkshire). However, the most innovative building was the work of the Bigods, one of the baronial families that gave Henry most trouble. They replaced their timber castle at FRAMLINGHAM (Suffolk) – an adulterine building dismantled by the King a few years earlier – with an imposing enceinte defended by 13 towers and, at a remarkably early date (the 1190s), omitting a keep.

All three of these advanced curtains carried rectangular mural towers; but rounded forms soon became much more common. These might be round, semi-circular or 'D'-plan; the latter was widely used in ambitious building schemes, since it combined a rounded front, projecting beyond the wall, with ample space and the more comfortable and convenient-to-organize rectangular room shape. Good examples of 13th-century curtain walls with rounded mural towers are found at BEESTON (Cheshire), PEVENSEY (East Sussex), HELMSLEY (North Yorkshire), DOVER (the outer curtain, built by King John), the TOWER OF LONDON (inner curtain) and the great castles of North Wales (described separately on pages 34–7).

As always, the most vulnerable point was the unavoidable gap in the castle wall created by the need for an entrance. During this period it was immensely strengthened by the development of the twin-towered gatehouse, which consisted of two mighty linked towers with a passageway between them; to pass through it, an attacker had to break down one or more doors and portcullises while being assaulted by missiles flung down through the *murder holes* (openings in the passage ceiling) and arrows shot through slits in the great chambers situated on the ground floor of each tower. A really strong (and expensive) castle might have more than one gatehouse as well as *posterns* or sallyports – much smaller gateways through which supplies might be received or members of the garrison might slip out, possibly to make an unexpected sortie against the enemy. Towards the end of the 13th century, gatehouses began to sport *machicolations*, which were projecting galleries with series of holes through which missiles could be dropped on the enemy. These stone equivalents to hoardings were soon being used in other parts of the castle, often to great decorative effect.

Further protection was afforded by a *barbican*. Developed earlier (the forebuilding was a kind of vertical barbican), this took many forms, but it was essentially a passage and/or courtyard through which the enemy had to pass in order to reach the gatehouse, being exposed to a variety of harassments and booby-traps.

Where possible, a moat was now added to the defences of the curtain. The siting of many castles made it impossible to keep the ditch or ditches filled with water, and elsewhere considerable resources were needed to undertake the necessary damming operations. However, in the 13th century spectacular water defences were created at KENILWORTH (Warwickshire), LEEDS (Kent), the TOWER

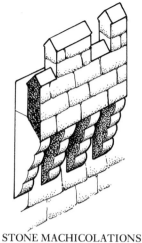

STONE MACHICOLATIONS

OTHER 13TH-CENTURY CASTLES
Apart from the many examples described and illustrated in this book, Skenfrith and Grosmont (both in Gwent) have classic round-towered curtains. Goodrich (Hereford and Worcester) is a magnificent ruin with a daunting barbican involving entry into an enclosure and a left turn up a set of steps to reach the gatehouse. Criccieth (Gwynedd) has a powerful gatehouse, characteristic of Edward I's building.

Caerlaverock Castle – the only triangular castle in Britain

OF LONDON, CAERLAVEROCK (Dumfries and Galloway) and CAERPHILLY (Mid Glamorgan). Unlike a ditch, a moat inhibited mining operations and kept the attackers and their weapons at a distance. After KENILWORTH, protected by what was virtually a lake, stood out against the royal forces for six months in 1266, this form of defence acquired great prestige.

THE GREAT CASTLES OF WALES

Norman penetration of Wales began within a few years of the Conquest. The newcomers occupied much of the south at an early date and acquired a far less secure grip on the northern coastline, while Snowdonia remained the heartland of Welsh resistance, providing a base for hit-and-run warfare as well as a refuge in defeat. In this permanent 'front-line' situation, both sides absorbed the latest innovations in warfare, including castle design. The initiative was not always in Norman hands, especially when it was possible for a shrewd Welsh leader to exploit the frequent periods of civil strife in 12th- and 13th-century England. During his long reign (1194–1240) Llywelyn ap Iowerth (Llywelyn the Great) made himself prince of all North Wales, extending his territories as far as Chester in Cheshire.

The situation was changed decisively by the English soldier-king Edward I (1272–1307), who conquered Wales and carried out a programme of castle-building on an unprecedented scale. All the most advanced 13th-century ideas were put into practice on Edward's castles, including the *concentric* layout. Essentially this involved putting up not one but two curtain walls, one outside and more or less parallel to the other. This was not just a matter of multiplying lines of defence, as had already been done at KENILWORTH (Warwickshire) and elsewhere. In the true concentric castle, the terrace or ward between the inner and outer curtain was quite narrow, and the outer curtain was lower than the inner one. This had two advantages: archers on the inner curtain could fire over the outer wall at the enemy beyond; and if the besiegers broke through into the terrace, they would find themselves in a cramped space where they could not make their superior numbers tell and where missiles rained down from both walls on their crowded ranks.

It has been suggested that various British military techniques and architectural ideas were brought back from the East by the crusaders, but in most instances it is hard to be sure that they were not simply independent discoveries. However, it does seem that huge concentric fortresses such as Krak des Chevaliers in Syria influenced Edward and his contemporaries, especially since the King was a widely travelled military enthusiast and crusader. Surprisingly, the very first concentric

REVERSE OF EDWARD I'S SEAL

Right *Beaumaris, a fine concentric castle*

castle in Britain was begun slightly earlier than Edward's, at CAERPHILLY (Mid Glamorgan) in South Wales by the immensely rich and powerful Marcher lord Gilbert de Clare. CAERPHILLY became the greatest private fortress ever built in Britain, incorporating spectacular water defences of the kind Gilbert had seen at the siege of KENILWORTH, round towers swollen to a massive 'drum' shape, and huge gatehouses. The largest and highest exemplified the already visible tendency for the keep to be reintroduced in a different form, as a 'keep-gatehouse', with ample accommodation, immense strength, and a design that enabled it to be sealed off and defended when the rest of the castle had fallen.

Edward's campaign in Wales began after Llywelyn ap Iowerth's grandson, Llywelyn ap Gruffydd (Llywelyn the Last, 1246–82), refused to acknowledge the English king as his overlord. In 1277 Edward invaded the north, drove the Welsh back, and began building royal castles at Flint and RHUDDLAN (Clwyd) even before a ruthless blockade of Snowdonia had forced Llywelyn to submit. Although there was as yet no direct occupation, the erection of six castles in Mid and North Wales made it clear that Edward was tightening his grip. And when his efforts to introduce English law led to a new war in 1282–3, Llywelyn was killed in a skirmish, and North Wales was annexed and reorganized into shires on the English model.

Simultaneously a second phase of castle-building was begun, including such famous royal foundations as CONWY, CAERNARFON and HARLECH (all in Gwynedd); after a further revolt in 1294, the building of BEAUMARIS on Anglesey (Gwynedd) re-emphasized the English will to dominate the country.

To this end, no less than 17 castles were built by or for Edward. Ten were new royal foundations; three were refortifications of Welsh strongholds; and four, including CHIRK (Clwyd), were 'lordship' castles, erected by English barons but funded from royal land grants and probably designed with the help of royal experts. The expense, vast by medieval standards and sustained over decades, was a measure of Edward's determination; the castle and city walls of CAERNARFON alone are reckoned to have cost £27,000. His object was to hem in Snowdonian Wales with an iron ring of mainly coastal castles which could be provisioned by sea in the event of an uprising. The major fortresses served a thoroughgoing colonial function, protecting equally new walled towns into which only English settlers were allowed; both the castle and walls have survived intact at CONWY and CAERNARFON, which are among the finest examples anywhere of this arrangement.

Although the great 'Edwardian' castles were all the work of Master James of St George, the King's Savoyard master mason, they are strikingly varied. Both CONWY and CAERNARFON were adapted to long sites, with a wall down the middle dividing each castle into two *wards* ('ward' tends to be used from the 13th century in preference to 'bailey', although the difference is purely verbal). CAERNARFON's

HARLECH'S SOUTH-WEST TOWER

OTHER WELSH CASTLES
Apart from those mentioned earlier, pre-Edwardian Norman castles in Wales include Penhow (Gwent), Cilgerran and Manorbier (both in Dyfed), and Coity (Mid Glamorgan). The best-preserved native Welsh castles are Dolbadarn (Gwynedd) and Ewloe (Clwyd); while Edward I 'modernized' the fortresses at Criccieth, Dolwyddelan and Castell y Bere (all in Gwynedd). Of the new castles built by Edward and not described in this book, Flint (Clwyd) has easily the most substantial remains, one of its large 'corner' towers being separated from the curtain and moated to serve as a keep. Among the 'lordship' castles are Hawarden and Denbigh (with contemporary town walls), both in Clwyd.

towers are polygonal, not round, and this, in combination with the coloured banding on the outside, makes it clear that the castle's function was partly symbolic, evoking the famous Theodosian walls of imperial Constantinople. By contrast, RHUDDLAN, HARLECH and BEAUMARIS are superb concentric castles; BEAUMARIS was the perfect example of the type, albeit too expensive to finish. All in all, the Edwardian castle represents the apotheosis of the medieval British fortress, built on a scale and with a technical efficiency that would never be surpassed.

TO BUILD A CASTLE

Once their distinctive arrangement and purpose have been understood, castles such as the TOWER OF LONDON and CAERPHILLY (Mid Glamorgan) can be seen as ranking with the finest building achievements of the Middle Ages. Like the great cathedrals, they represent wonderfully sustained and skilful labours, executed with a very limited technology: a range of simple digging, cutting, prising and hammering tools, one or two more sophisticated instruments such as the set square and mason's level, and a few devices using the treadmill, windlass or block and tackle.

Medieval man had little interest in making written records of such humdrum affairs, and most of what we know comes from a handful of manuscript illustrations and some more abundant financial records. The records were almost exclusively compiled by the royal accountants, so it is as well to remember that most lords, having thrown up a timber castle at some point after the Norman Conquest, were unable to afford large-scale building programmes and made any further changes piecemeal, perhaps over several decades of carefully budgeted activity. The surviving records, which in many instances show strong-minded kings pressing forward regardless of obstacles, are to that extent misleading.

Castle sites were chosen for a mixture of strategic, political and social reasons, of course with due consideration for the nature of the terrain. Although bedrock might be ideal, where necessary foundations were dug, timber was driven into the soil to strengthen it, or a motte was provided with a stone core to support the weight of the building above it. If the castle to be built was to be large and ambitiously designed, the operations involved called for extremely efficient organization to ensure that quantities of materials and large numbers of men were on site at the appropriate time. A stone castle required plenty of timber (temporary accommodation and scaffolding for the workforce; floors and roof-beams for the castle); sand, lime and water for mortar; and perhaps plaster for the interiors, glass for the windows and lead for the chimney flues. Given the difficulty of transporting heavy goods, stone was brought from the nearest quarry, or earlier

A COAT OF ARMS

37

A MEDIEVAL MASTER MASON

Left *The White Tower at the heart of the Tower of London*

buildings on the site were plundered. However, for a high-quality finish, stone was imported over a long period from Caen in Normandy.

Many lords must have recruited their labour force locally, bringing only the necessary specialists from any great distance. By contrast, when Edward I initiated his great Welsh castle-building campaign in 1277, men were summoned – in effect conscripted – from all over England and even from the King's French possessions. Their numbers reached about 3000, of whom almost two-thirds were diggers – an indication of the immense change in the landscape made by large-scale clearing, levelling and ditching with pick and shovel. Among others employed were masons to cut and lay the stones, carpenters, blacksmiths, hod-carriers, charcoal-burners and general labourers. As the most skilled men, the masons were paid two shillings a week; the more or less unskilled received between eightpence and a shilling.

Obviously the architects in charge of important royal buildings were skilled men; and the records tell us some of their names. Work at the TOWER OF LONDON and ROCHESTER CASTLE (Kent), and perhaps also COLCHESTER (Essex), was directed by Gundulf, Bishop of Rochester, whom a contemporary describes as 'very competent and skilful at building in stone'; as an ecclesiastic, able to read, he may have consulted ancient Roman writings on fortification. He must also have depended on a master mason, the nearest thing to a professional architect during the Middle Ages. Henry II's master mason, 'Maurice the Engineer', built the royal castles at DOVER (Kent) and Newcastle (Tyne and Wear); and an even more important figure, Master James of St George, was responsible for all of Edward I's great Welsh castles. The King imported Master James specially from Savoy and, evidently recognizing his exceptional qualities, gave him the title Master of the King's Works in Wales, paid him the unprecedented wage of three shillings a day, and eventually appointed him constable in charge of one of his major castles, HARLECH (Gwynedd). Unfortunately, although his castles reveal a genius for design and adaptation, and even a penchant for experiment, nothing is known of the training or working methods of Master James, although we can be fairly certain that he was an expert draughtsman with a thorough grasp of number, proportion and geometry.

On arriving at PEVENSEY (East Sussex), William the Conqueror seems to have put up his prefabricated castle in a matter of, at most, days; and one of the advantages of the post-Conquest timber motte-and-bailey castles was that they could be built within a single season. But stone castles took years to build, the workforce assembling and dispersing summer after summer. (In winter there was a danger that frost would crack the mortar while it was still drying.) Early Norman masonry can be identified by the courses of diagonally set stones; the alternating diagonals give this *herringbone* pattern its distinctive vertical zigzag effect. Herringbone patches can often be spotted in stretches of otherwise rebuilt wall, for example at RICHMOND (North Yorkshire). The walls of most English castles were faced with *ashlar* (smooth, squared-off blocks of stone) outside and in, with a mass of rubble (irregular stones and mortar) filling the space between to give the necessary thickness and strength. As the walls rose higher, the work was continued from the platforms of timber scaffolding, but a new and effective Savoyard technique was used to build the great round Edwardian towers of Wales: spiral scaffolding, supported by horizontal beams fixed into the completed area of the tower. Seven hundred years later, the square 'putlog' holes that held the beams can still be seen, moving diagonally around Master James's towers.

This type of evidence is worth looking for in castles, most of which have been stripped down by time to their basic military virtue – the mighty walls of tower, gatehouse and curtain. But although medieval portcullises have disappeared, the grooves which they slid down are still there, as are the holes along the wallhead for the beams that supported hoardings, and the recesses into which long-vanished drawbridges swung; and so are the changes of shade and shape in the masonry where one season's building ended and another began – or, even more exciting, the outlines of battlements sealed in a wall which has been heightened as a result of some later decision, as at COLCHESTER and ROTHESAY (Strathclyde). To be on the alert for such things is to increase appreciably the pleasure of visiting a great castle.

THE CASTLE IN PEACETIME

Unless it stood on hotly contested border territory, the castle was likely to be a peaceful residence for far longer periods than those in which it saw service as a military headquarters or beleaguered fortress. So it is not surprising to find comfort, display and other non-military considerations competing for attention and ultimately conflicting with the requirements of defence. In time, this would lead to the phasing out of the castle in favour of purely civilian domiciles such as the country house and the palace.

As a lordly residence – even one visited only occasionally – the castle needed to be not only comfortable but an appropriate setting in which its master could do justice, administer his estates and demonstrate his wealth and power by entertaining dependants and guests in high style. Even the external appearance of his castle would have been less dour than it now seems, thanks to the coat of whitewash that it was commonly given; and it would be surprising if the strips, arcades and other relief decorations on London's White (washed) Tower, CASTLE RISING (Norfolk) and other mighty fortresses were not picked out in colour to make them stand out. Moreover, although the almost complete disappearance of original castle roofs makes it impossible to dogmatize, it seems likely that many

The great hall of Berkeley Castle, seen from the dais

of them were cone-shaped, in which case they would have had something of the 'fairy-tale' air characteristic of so many Scottish and French castles.

Despite a gradual improvement in the amenities of life, the basic arrangements within the medieval castle remained remarkably constant. A large, lofty hall served as the main public setting in which the lord appeared – to dine in state, to do justice, to preside over the rituals of chivalry. On such an occasion the lord and his family would occupy a dais at one end of the hall. At the other, behind a screen, lay the pantry and buttery; the pantry (from the French *pain*, 'bread') was the dry-goods store, the buttery (French *bouteille*, 'bottle') for liquors. The kitchens were often sited at a distance, either to keep cooking smells away from the hall, or because of the fire risk represented by large-scale ox-spitting operations. Medieval kitchens have survived at DURHAM and RABY (both in County Durham), and DOUNE (Central) boasts a separate kitchen tower.

Flour, salted meat and fish, and other non-perishable foodstuffs could be stored on the bottom floor of the keep; apart from the suitability of these almost window-less rooms for storage, this ensured that even the most unexpected attack need not lead to instant capitulation. (For the same reason, one of the castle's wells was always sited in the keep.) Incidentally, the idea that the lower rooms of castles were 'dungeons' is unfounded: the word itself is a version of *donjon*, an alternative name for a keep, and probably derived from the much later (18th- and 19th-century) use of defunct castles as prisons. During the Middle Ages, prisoners of noble or gentle birth would generally have been accommodated in a fashion suitable to their rank, while prisoners of any other kind would probably not have been taken in the first place.

A desire for privacy made itself felt through the provision of an increasing number of private chambers, beginning with a *solar* for the lord's family, situated behind the hall or over the pantry and buttery. In this, as in other respects, the keep reproduced these arrangements, stacking the rooms vertically (except for the divisions made possible by a cross-wall) rather than horizontally. The first-floor hall might rise through two storeys, or there might be two halls, one above the other, for the castellan or constable and his visiting lord. Private chambers were placed in the upper storeys or cut into the thickness of the wall, as was often also done with stairs and galleries.

A few castle keeps were literally places of last resort, never used except in an emergency. This reflected the growing importance of the bailey, which – even before the development of the strong curtain wall – tended to have extra accommodation as well as such auxiliary functions as workshops and stables. In most instances this duplication meant that, in peacetime, the keep (and later its gate-house equivalent) became the lord's private residence, a splendid great hall in the bailey being used for all the public business of lordship. In the later Middle Ages, as hospitality and client-dependant relationships became important,

A 12TH-CENTURY DOORWAY

CHIRK'S WATCH-TOWER STAIRCASE

individual lodgings multiplied, sometimes (as at CAISTER, Norfolk) catering for relatively humble retainers and servants.

There were other absolutely indispensable items in the medieval castle. One was the chapel, for even the blackest-hearted barons and mercenaries thought of themselves as Christians. There was always a chapel in the keep as well as one in the bailey; sometimes there were even two keep chapels, one of them exclusive to the king or lord. Fine castle chapels survive from all periods, from William I's at DURHAM to the late medieval St George's Chapel at WINDSOR (Berkshire). The other indispensables were lavatories (variously called latrines, privies and garderobes), built into the thickness of the wall or sited in a designated latrine tower, as at Coity in Mid Glamorgan. Castle latrines can be surprisingly well designed and numerous, as for example at BEAUMARIS (Gwynedd).

Like its outside, the interior of a castle was probably more colourful and cheerful than is suggested by the bare, chill stonework of the present day. The furniture would certainly have been sparse and heavy – mainly wooden chests, tables and cupboards – but the floor would have been covered with rushes sweetened with herbs from the castle garden; and plasterwork, tapestries, painted decoration and perhaps carpets from the East would have enlivened the walls. The blazing fire in a central hearth would have been a mixed blessing, the smoke accumulating in the room until it drifted sluggishly through a vent in the ceiling; and despite early examples of fireplaces (COLCHESTER, Essex; ROCHESTER, Kent) and chimneys (HEDINGHAM CASTLE, Essex), these did not become common until the 14th century. Glass, too, replaced shutters only slowly; its installation, and the growing size of windows, were signs that the castle was beginning to lose its military virtue and change into the country house.

———◆———

THE QUEST FOR SECURITY

It is tempting to contrast the great Edward I, conqueror of Wales and 'Hammer of the Scots', with his weak son Edward II (1307–27), who was defeated by the Scots at Bannockburn, failed to master the baronial opposition at home, and was ultimately deposed and murdered. But in reality the Crown had already fallen into difficulties during the later part of Edward I's reign as a result of the King's wars against Scotland and France, and as early as 1297–8 unpopular taxes led to a serious internal crisis. It is arguable that the ruinous cost of Edward's wars and castles had a crippling effect on the royal finances and general social stability whose effects were felt throughout the final two centuries of the Middle Ages.

Although he could defeat and savage the Scots, Edward was unable to hold

OTHER CASTLES WITH
NOTABLE DOMESTIC
FEATURES
Castell Coch (South Glamorgan) was largely rebuilt by the 19th-century architect William Burges; it represents a serious attempt to re-create a small 13th-century castle – complete with speculative but plausible conical roofs. Longthorpe Tower (Cambridgeshire) is of exceptional interest because of its 14th-century wall paintings of biblical scenes.

Stokesay Castle – an authentic example of a medieval fortified manor

them down for long, since he could not afford to embark on a second hugely expensive programme of castle-building. As a result of this failure, Anglo-Scottish hostilities flared up at regular intervals over the next two and a half centuries, and there was endemic, almost unbroken cross-border violence – lawless raiding and robbing which made life insecure for both Scots and northern English. On the English side, one consequence was the development of new Marcher lords with dangerously large private armies and splendid, quasi-regal castles: the Percy Earls of Northumberland at ALNWICK and WARKWORTH (both in Northumberland), and the Neville Earls of Westmorland at RABY (County Durham).

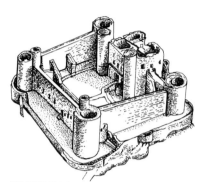

HARLECH CASTLE – AERIAL VIEW

Another consequence was the proliferation of pele (or peel) towers on both sides of the border between the 14th and 17th centuries. These were homely versions of the great keep – relatively small, sturdy, usually rectangular tower houses built by the gentry or even humbler folk; only a few, such as SIZERGH (Cumbria), were of any great size or were dignified with battlements, machicolations or turrets. Usually a pele tower stood within an enclosure, or barmkin, surrounded by a plain wall that served as a cattle pen rather than a serious form of defence. The residents of the pele, like those of the keep, relied on thick walls to keep the enemy at bay – a rational policy, since raiders generally looked for quick gains (loot or cattle), descending on a settlement and then retiring at speed before the locality could be raised against them. Since the overwhelming majority of English peles were put up in the four northernmost counties, it is clear that they were specifically a response to border conditions.

CONWY'S WEST BARBICAN

Elsewhere in England and Wales, another kind of sub-castle seems to have become more common. This was the fortified manor, which owed its courtesy title of castle to a licence to crenellate and a limited amount of new building such as the addition of a tower and moat to an existing hall-house; a celebrated early example (1291) is STOKESAY (Shropshire). The difficulty of discovering the grass-roots reality of medieval society is shown by the fact that the fortification of a number of manors around 1300 can be given opposite interpretations: as a response by peaceful householders to growing lawlessness and social tensions, or as expressing a feeling of security on the part of people who might earlier have built in a more thoroughly martial fashion. Certainly, dwellings such as STOKESAY could only hope to withstand or repel a small-scale attack, and in many instances the fortifications of manor houses give the impression of being little more than martial flourishes. Since even humble farmhouses were more often being given some form of primitive protection – usually just a surrounding ditch – it may be that burglary rather than feudal disorder was perceived as a threat in a society suffering from overpopulation and inflation.

Since the castle proper had reached its apogee as a military machine under Edward I, few significant improvements were made to it during the 14th century. In fact, Edwardian designs on the grandest scale were not to be seen again. Instead, castle-builders emphasized particular elements – the mighty gatehouse or the lofty tower – or opted for a courtyard castle, modelled in a general way on quadrangular Edwardian castles such as HARLECH (Gwynedd), but with ranges of buildings along the four sides offering ample accommodation. In the castles of the great, a premium was now put on ostentatious display, hospitality and comfort, even at the expense of military efficiency.

Not many true castles were built in the first half of the 14th century, although several existing ones were brought up to date, acquiring new gatehouses or barbicans; KIDWELLY (Dyfed) was even converted into a concentric castle of an unusual kind. Significantly, the most powerful new fortress, DUNSTANBURGH (Northumberland), was the work of Thomas, Earl of Lancaster, leader of the baronial opposition to Edward II.

During the 14th century the magnates of the realm re-emerged as men of power whose numerous retainers and network of dependants and clients constituted a potential threat to royal authority. This development has been labelled 'bastard feudalism', since the relationship between a lord and his followers, once exclusively centred on land-holding, was now increasingly based on cash. The employment of mercenaries has been offered as an explanation for the accentuated tendency of lords to maintain a wholly self-sufficient residence in a gatehouse or tower which could be sealed off from an unreliable garrison. However, a desire for privacy, a wish to emphasize distinctions of rank, and a pride in opulently duplicating every castle function may have been at least as important. Such motives would become common enough in the age of rapacious warfare and chivalric splendour that began in the late 14th century.

AN AGE OF CHIVALRY AND WAR

Under Edward III (1327–77) there was a new boom in castle-building, thanks to the high state and self-conscious pageantry adopted by both the King and his magnates. The boom was to a considerable extent financed – and motivated – by the war with France which broke out in 1337 and has become known as the Hundred Years War. The name is not fully justified, since the period between 1337 and 1453 really witnessed a series of Anglo-French wars broken by intervals during which peace or a long truce prevailed. On the other hand, the 'war' does have a kind of unity, since it represented a fairly sustained effort by English kings to assert their claim to the French throne or, more realistically, to win and hold substantial territories in France; and the final expulsion of the invaders ended an era in French history and plunged English society into crisis.

In its early years, one effect of the war was to generate patriotic feeling and

Right The ruined interior of the great hall at Kenilworth Castle, looking eastwards

channel the energies of the magnates into foreign adventures; but in the long run it probably strengthened their position at home, since the recruiting system made them the leaders and paymasters of bodies of troops whose first loyalty was to their noble masters. What mattered immediately, however, was the spectacular success of Edward's early campaigns, crowned by famous victories at Crécy (1346) and Poitiers (1356). On occasions such as these, and in many minor skirmishes for decades to come, there were rich pickings to be had in the way of loot and, above all, ransoms. And not just for the magnate: the knight who managed to capture a great French noble might well find that he had made his fortune at a stroke. Moreover, given the extraordinary and prolonged nature of the war effort, advancement was still more likely for the indefatigable administrator and organizer. Consequently, there were many 14th- and 15th-century veterans who returned from the wars much richer than their forebears and, in an increasingly status-conscious society, eager to display the fact even in their retirement.

The castles they proceeded to build were often influenced by what they had seen abroad, as at NUNNEY (Somerset), with its close, tall towers and French-style continuous line of machicolations, and OLD WARDOUR (Wiltshire), a remarkable hexagonal structure built round a courtyard. Incidentally, a 17th-century sketch of NUNNEY has been preserved which proves that its roof towers were cone-capped, making it still more 'French' in appearance. Such luxurious 'tower house' castles (not to be confused with the small, functional tower houses of northern Britain) represented one method of self-aggrandizement. Another was adopted at DONNINGTON (Berkshire) by Sir Richard Abberbury, who built the splendid gatehouse, visible from afar, which is all that now remains of the courtyard castle.

In the south, castles were also built, and town walls fortified, for purposes of national defence; the French had raided the south coast to great effect in 1338, and a repetition was feared even at the height of English success in France. The King himself saw to the fortification of the Thames Estuary, building a perfectly circular concentric castle at Queenborough in Kent. It was the only major royal castle put up during his reign, and evidently very advanced in design, but unfortunately it has completely disappeared. Elsewhere the Crown was able to economize by licensing status-hungry subjects to fortify their properties. The best known of these was BODIAM (East Sussex), another castle built with war profits. It is one of the most beautiful of English castles and a classic example of the southern courtyard style, with its great round angle towers, imposing gatehouse and barbican, and broad moat. Its military effectiveness is another matter, not easy to evaluate; for, in this as in other instances, there is a puzzling contradiction between weaknesses such as the invitingly big windows and the elaborate and surely serious entrance defences. By contrast, BOLTON CASTLE (North Yorkshire) maintains the northern tradition of rectangular towers and dispenses with a gatehouse, although not with the provision of completely separate quarters for the lord.

A KNIGHT IN ARMOUR *c.* 1325

The most spectacular 14th-century castles reflect the cult of chivalry that developed during Edward III's reign. This was compounded of sumptuous pageantry, constantly elaborated ceremonial, conspicuous heraldic display and a mystique of blue-blooded behaviour based on fantasies of knight-errantry and love as practised by King Arthur and other legendary heroes; one of the most celebrated cultic, élitist manifestations of the chivalric idea was the founding of the Order of the Garter by Edward himself. Although doubtless fuelled by the great English victories in France (in which the common longbowmen played an important and notably unchivalric part), this was a widespread European development which gave court life in the late Middle Ages its distinctively strange and gorgeous air. Impelled by his self-image as the chivalric beau ideal, Edward made his birthplace, WINDSOR (Berkshire), into a superb castle of chivalry, amplifying and adorning it in – literally – palatial style without significantly improving its fighting capability; and his son, John of Gaunt, followed suit at KENILWORTH (Warwickshire), where the noble ruin of the great hall still exhibits wonderfully carved stonework and majestic windows. At WARWICK CASTLE (Warwickshire) another magnate, Thomas Beauchamp, did combine military effectiveness with chivalric display, transforming the old castle by building a new east front with a strong, visually splendid and unusual tower (Caesar's Tower and Guy's Tower) at each end. The great northern strongholds of the Percys and Nevilles (mentioned earlier on page 45) were also castles of chivalry.

Edward's reign ended in defeat and disillusion, but chivalric ostentation, like the mirage of French conquest, persisted into the 15th century.

(mentioned earlier on page 45)

OTHER 14TH-CENTURY CASTLES
Knaresborough (North Yorkshire) is a tower house built early in the century, as is Dudley (West Midlands), much restored and entertainingly sited at the heart of a zoo. By contrast, the tower house at Hylton (Tyne and Wear) dates from the end of the century.
Quadrangular castles include Farleigh Hungerford (Somerset), Lumley (County Durham) and the Neville stronghold of Sheriff Hutton (North Yorkshire).

THE END OF ENGLISH CASTLE-BUILDING

After a series of social and dynastic crises in the late 14th century, England appeared to have been united by Henry V (1413–22), the victor of Agincourt, who again brought much of France under English rule. Henry's early death left a minor, Henry VI (1422–61; 1470–1), on the throne, and faction and intrigue persisted throughout the long, ultimately disastrous wars in France (to 1453) and almost immediately afterwards broke out into the dynastic civil wars known as the Wars of the Roses (1455–85).

Despite the turbulence and apparent insecurity of 15th-century life, there was an emphatic slump in castle-building. Of course, this may have meant only that saturation-point had been reached as far as the Crown and the higher nobility were concerned. Certainly the important new castles were all put up by men who had risen in the world thanks to the fortunes of war or civil war; and what they built were – even more obviously than their 14th-century equivalents – unashamed

St Mawes Castle, an artillery fort built by Henry VIII in Cornwall

A 15TH-CENTURY SIEGE-GUN

show-castles advertising their new greatness. Brick was now a highly fashionable material, particularly suitable for ostentatious building on account of its rich red-ness and capacity for striking patterning. At TATTERSHALL (Lincolnshire), CAISTER (Norfolk) and KIRBY MUXLOE (Leicestershire) this was combined with other features mainly for show, such as pronounced machicolations, polygonal turrets and highly visible personal and heraldic devices. Boasting a large tower or gate-house, and surrounded by a moat, a building of this kind was defensible for a time, as was demonstrated in 1469 by a well-known affray at CAISTER, which held out for a couple of weeks against the Duke of Norfolk's men. (However, they were asserting their master's dubious claim to the property, and may have been instructed not to inflict too much damage on it!) But this was quite another matter from taking any part in full-scale warfare (which none of these castles ever did). An even grander, and perhaps more genuinely warlike, stone castle was RAGLAN (Gwent), its two courtyards and separate hexagonal tower for the lord representing a mighty flourish on the part of the fast-rising Herbert family, distinguished in the French wars and pillars of the Yorkist cause in the Wars of the Roses.

Significantly, pele towers continued to be built in the North, and fortified manor houses such as HEVER (Kent) were maintained or even strengthened. But many castles proper had already been abandoned and allowed to decay; one traveller, William Worcester, noted several dozen of these in 1479–80, including such well-known names as BEESTON (Cheshire), HEDINGHAM (Essex), NORWICH (Norfolk), PORTCHESTER (Hampshire) and TINTAGEL (Cornwall). Such older castles were evidently too remote or too uncomfortable for late medieval tastes.

A more surprising fact is that fully operational castles played little part in the Wars of the Roses, although in the French wars Englishmen had become accustomed to almost unbroken siege warfare. On home ground both sides chose to seek a quick victory on the battlefield, perhaps because such positive action was felt to be essential in securing the allegiance – and the taxes – of the uncommit-ted majority; and since the vendetta-like atmosphere of the wars ensured that high-born prisoners would be murdered instead of ransomed, the participants had no reason to spin out the proceedings. There were a few sieges, notably at HARLECH (Gwynedd) and BAMBURGH (Northumberland), which in 1464 became the first British castle to be taken as a result of a bombardment by artillery.

Efforts were made to adapt some older castles to this form of warfare by widen-ing their arrow-slits into *gunports* (apertures through which guns could be fired), and 15th-century castles such as CAISTER and KIRBY MUXLOE were provided with gunports from the beginning. But generally speaking such measures were badly conceived or perhaps merely perfunctory, and nothing else of note was done to overcome the disadvantages of the castle (the lack of space for big guns, the lofti-ness that made it an easy target), despite the fact that when BAMBURGH fell, gun-powder had already been in use for over a century.

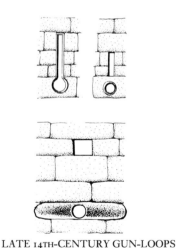

LATE 14TH-CENTURY GUN-LOOPS

A statue of Robert the Bruce at Stirling Castle

In other words, enthusiasm for the castle as a fighting machine had begun to wane long before artillery became formidable, and was related to a rapidly dwindling enthusiasm for living in such machines. Far earlier than their Continental (or Scottish) counterparts, the English nobility were either abandoning their castles for, or converting them into, the comfortable country houses that were to remain the norm for upper-class living down to the 20th century. The process was so advanced by the late 16th century that, as the scholar Sir Thomas Wilson forthrightly declared, 'in England there is no great reckoning made of castles and fortresses, for they do willingly let them go to ruin and instead thereof build them stately pleasant houses and palaces'.

However, the palace-building Tudor king Henry VIII (1509–47) also created an impressive chain of fortresses, although these were not true castles: that is, not personal possessions but state institutions; not dwellings but artillery forts garrisoned by professional soldiers; and not lofty symbols of lordship but low gun platforms grouped around a squat central tower. Nevertheless, they are castles by title and are eminently visitable, with petal-like or lobate designs that are at their most elegant at DEAL (Kent) and ST MAWES (Cornwall), while Elizabethan UPNOR (Kent), with its riverside setting, is also visually exciting. By this time, English military men had grasped the importance of the Continental system of arrowhead *bastions* (gun platforms thrusting right out into enemy 'field' from the defensive centre), which were used to strengthen one castle, CARISBROOKE (Isle of Wight), and, on a breathtaking scale, to fortify an entire city, Berwick-upon-Tweed. But such devices belonged essentially to a new age of military science in which the castle apparently had no place.

———————◆———————

THE SCOTTISH TRADITION

Scotland is without exaggeration a land rich in castles: wherever you are, there will be at least one worth visiting that can be reached with no very great effort. Scottish life remained turbulent and uncertain for much longer than was the case in England, and as a result castles remained in use, continued to be built, and were lived in for an equivalently long period, right down to the 17th century. Many have survived essentially unspoiled and have been continuously inhabited for centuries.

There were various types of stone fortresses – brochs and duns – around 2000 years ago in the far north and Hebrides. But the medieval type of castle was introduced into Scotland, along with feudalism, from the late 11th century. This has been described as a 'bloodless Norman conquest', for the Scottish kings of the Canmore dynasty encouraged immigration from the south, and by the 12th

OTHER 15TH- AND 16TH-CENTURY CASTLES

Baconsthorpe (Norfolk) is a well-preserved fortified manor house of the mid 15th century with a strong gatehouse and moat. Herstmonceux (East Sussex), unfortunately not open to the public at present, is a classic brick show-castle. Henrican forts still in good condition include Walmer (Kent); St Mawes' partner, Pendennis (Cornwall); Hurst (Hampshire), fascinating because of its position, far out in the Solent; and Yarmouth (Isle of Wight), square in plan and very up to date (for an English fort) in being equipped with an arrowhead bastion.

century there was an Anglo-Norman ruling class occupying great fiefs in the Scottish Lowlands and owing feudal services and allegiance to the Scottish king. Like their English counterparts they put up motte-and-bailey castles before beginning to use stone, but this development was relatively slow, and only a handful of really ambitious fortresses had been built before the pivotal event in Scottish history occurred: the struggle against England for national independence.

During the early feudal period Anglo-Scottish conflicts were relatively infrequent and brief, and there was a long period of peace during the 13th century. Although English claims to suzerainty remained unresolved, Scotland's kings had more pressing problems at home: expelling the Norsemen from the west coast and holding them at bay with castles such as ROTHESAY (Strathclyde), and trying to extend royal control into the wild, recalcitrant Highlands.

The great crisis occurred because the Scottish royal line became extinct in 1290. Edward I of England, now master of Wales, was accepted as overlord and arbiter between the rival claimants to the vacant throne. He chose John Baliol; but Baliol soon failed to carry out his feudal obligations – as Edward conceived them – and the angry English king invaded Scotland in 1295. Baliol was defeated, but in spite of Edward's military advantages Scottish resistance to English rule flared up again and again. An epic struggle developed in which there were many sieges, culminating in the investment of STIRLING (Central) in 1304. English records reveal that this was a major operation involving wooden bridges prefabricated in Norfolk and transported all the way to Scotland, a belfry, and various siege engines including something referred to as a 'war wolf'; it was ready for action when the Scots offered to surrender – an offer Edward refused to accept until he had taken a shot at the castle with his new weapon!

But Edward never managed to consolidate his position in Scotland, partly because he could not afford to replicate his Welsh castle-building programme. The Scots were certainly aware of the aggressive, territory-securing role played by castles after the Conquest and in Wales, for they *slighted* (made indefensible) their own as well as captured fortresses, evidently judging that their defensive potential in Scots hands was far less significant than their usefulness to the occupying power. CAERLAVEROCK (Dumfries and Galloway), EDINBURGH (Lothian) and STIRLING were among these self-slighted castles; and these and other events in Scottish history explain why the buildings on superb defensive sites such as those occupied by EDINBURGH and STIRLING are relatively late in date.

Under Robert the Bruce the Scots defeated Edward II at Bannockburn (1314) and took the initiative. There followed centuries of disastrous official and unofficial warfare across the border. Scotland was habitually associated with France in 'the auld alliance', which exposed her to fresh cultural influences but also encouraged her to enter wars against a fundamentally much stronger England. Although Scottish independence was not seriously threatened, a series of military disasters from

CAERLAVEROCK – AERIAL VIEW

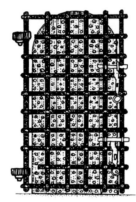

YETT AT CRATHES CASTLE

Right *Tantallon Castle, with the Bass Rock beyond*

Halidon Hill (1333) to Flodden (1513) undermined the state. Moreover, Scottish kings were extraordinarily accident-prone, spending years in captivity in England, being killed in battle or (as happened to James II in 1460) being blown up during a siege when a cannon exploded. Consequently, minorities and regencies helped to keep the state weak, and in the 14th century great baronial castles such as TANTALLON (Lothian) and DOUNE (Central) proclaimed that their owners were every bit as good as the Stuart kings.

Until this time, Scottish castle architecture had gone through much the same phases as its English equivalent, but in the course of the 14th century their paths diverged. The Scots now began to put up tower houses – structures like the English peles, but built not only on the devastated border territories but all over the country and by all classes. Essentially the tower house was a version of the keep, but like its northern English relative it was smaller and lacked such refinements as a forebuilding and a defended bailey containing extra buildings. It was a permanent all-year-round residence, entered at first-floor level by outside steps, or sometimes on the ground floor through a *yett*, a hinged iron grille of a kind also used in northern England.

For centuries this fortified tower house was the norm in Scotland. At HERMITAGE (Borders) it was superimposed on an earlier courtyard castle, and the rectangular towers of DRUM (Grampian), CAWDOR (Highland), THREAVE (Dumfries and Galloway), LOCH LEVEN and EDZELL (both in Tayside) cover some 200 years of building. Where more space was needed, a compact extra wing was added, giving an 'L'-plan, as at GLAMIS (Tayside) and DUNNOTTAR (Grampian), and much later at CRATHES and CRAIGIEVAR (both in Grampian). By the time these last two houses were built (in the late 16th and early 17th centuries) the tower-house building tradition had reached extraordinary heights of skill and sophistication, the plain lower floors flowering into delightful skylines with characteristic cone-capped projecting turrets, or *bartizans*, supported on *corbels* (brackets). Thus the dour, functional defended house became Scotland's great contribution to European architecture – a splendid final flourish before the castle gave way in the late 17th century to the mansion and palace.

SLIGHTINGS, SHAMS AND STATELY HOMES

By the late 16th century, fortresses were going out of fashion even in the North of England, one symptom being the conversion of a pele such as SIZERGH (Cumbria) into a comfortable country house. In 1603 the Stuart king James VI of Scotland inherited the English throne as James I, and the border apparently ceased to be a war zone. In the long run this proved to be true, but between

OTHER SCOTTISH CASTLES
This can be no more than a selection. Castle Sween (Highland) has claims to be Scotland's earliest medieval castle. Kildrummy (Grampian), Dirleton (Lothian), and Bothwell (Strathclyde) with its huge keep were substantial castles dating from before the Wars of Independence. Blackness (Central) exemplifies a 15th-century castle (even now with an ancient yett) adapted to use by artillery. The palaces at Falkland (Fife) and Linlithgow (Lothian) preserve evidence of their castle origins. Scotland's wealth of tower houses includes Castle Campbell (Central), the 'L'-plan Craigmillar (Lothian) and Muchalls (Grampian), and Claypotts (Tayside) and Castle Fraser (Grampian), built on the still more sophisticated 'Z'-plan, with a tower in each of the two diagonally-opposite corners of the main block. Ingeniously, at Huntingtower (Tayside) the space between two 15th-century tower houses was filled in to create a single mansion.

A carved angel in the roof of the great hall at Cardiff Castle

1639 and 1650 political and religious disputes led to the Civil War between King and Parliament in England, and also to conflicts between the English and the Scots, who first resisted and later supported the Stuarts.

Castles played a surprisingly important part in all this. Garrisons moved into those that were still inhabited and also occupied many which had been abandoned but had survived as strong, overgrown stone shells. Strengthened by up-to-date earthworks against the impact of cannonballs, these were often the scene of heroic and protracted sieges (for example at DONNINGTON, Berkshire), further evidence that the 15th- and 16th-century abandonment of castles had not been dictated by purely military motives. Nevertheless, the Civil War period caused a tremendous acceleration of the decline. Most English castles were held by the losing Royalist side and, apart from being assaulted, were slighted – disabled or even demolished – after the war, sometimes in revenge for their owners' activities and sometimes because this was cheaper than garrisoning them against a new Royalist effort. Castles in solidly Parliamentarian East Anglia and coastal fortresses such as ARUNDEL (West Sussex) and BODIAM (East Sussex) were spared, but DONNINGTON, CORFE (Dorset), HELMSLEY (North Yorkshire), KENILWORTH (Warwickshire), OLD WARDOUR (Wiltshire), SCARBOROUGH (North Yorkshire) and many others were seriously damaged.

After the Restoration of Charles II in 1660, some castles were wholly (BERKELEY, Gloucestershire) or partly (KENILWORTH) reoccupied, and at places such as CHIRK (Clwyd) and ROCKINGHAM (Northamptonshire) fortunes were spent in converting the old fortresses into luxurious homes. From now on there would be few military alarms, although early in the 18th century the Jacobite risings in support of the exiled Stuarts spelled disaster for castles such as EILEAN DONAN (Highland), DUNNOTTAR and Kildrummy (both in Grampian). Others were either extended and remodelled – often, but not always, at the expense of their original character – or, after a more or less protracted afterlife as prisons, courts or barracks, became part of a long, slow decay that only began to be stemmed in the 19th century.

One of the most curious things about castles is that their power and authority in the world of the imagination were unaffected by their dwindling significance in the real world. A battlemented martial air manifested itself in all sorts of places, beginning with the great gatehouses of Tudor abbeys and houses, which were actually only entrance lodges on an absurdly extravagant scale, and on the façades of such otherwise conspicuously palatial and unmilitary buildings as the 'prodigy houses' built by the Elizabethan élite.

At a remarkably early date there were people who went further, feeling the essentially romantic urge to build and live in a 'medieval' castle – one that was discreetly equipped with all the comforts of a later age and not in any sense intended for self-defence. The 'keep' at BOLSOVER (Derbyshire), built early in

BODIAM CASTLE'S BARBICAN

the 17th century, is unmistakably a flight of antiquarian fantasy despite its fidelity to the medieval arrangement of the rooms; it is the first – and at this date exceptional – example of a type of building that is rather unkindly termed a 'sham castle'.

Generally speaking, 18th-century landowners had a lighter-hearted and less respectful view of the Middle Ages, often incorporating castle ruins into a folly or carefully arranged picturesque view, as at OLD WARDOUR. But the late 18th-century Romantic movement created a new taste for a period variously seen as epitomizing chivalry, faith and artistic excellence; and in architecture more or less accurate versions of the medieval pointed-arched Gothic style were used on new churches, railway stations – and 'castles'. EASTNOR (Hereford and Worcester) represents one such response; CARDIFF (South Glamorgan) another. In Scotland some resplendent sham castles were built in a 'Scottish baronial' style derived from the more glamorous tower houses, often embellished with a luxurious French 'château' look; INVERARAY (Strathclyde) is an early example of this style, which gained a widespread urban and suburban popularity.

The 19th century was an era in which huge amounts were spent on refurbishing historic castles such as ARUNDEL and building palatial country houses, whether they were modelled as sham castles or 'Jacobethan' mansions. It also marked the beginning of conscientious efforts to conserve and restore older castles: by Lord Craven at STOKESAY (Shropshire), for example, and the Marquis of Bute at CAERPHILLY (Mid Glamorgan), followed in the 20th century by Viscount Astor at HEVER (Kent) and Lord Curzon at BODIAM and TATTERSHALL (Lincolnshire). In retrospect, such activities were invaluable in preserving national treasures until a wider sense of communal reponsibility developed and was embodied in the state and organizations such as the National Trust.

Ironically, the soot and steam of the Industrial Revolution made possible the great upsurge of building and rebuilding in the 19th century, pouring seemingly limitless wealth into the hands of industrialists and landowners who used much of it to realize arcadian and feudal fantasies. Significantly, the process hardly survived World War I. One new sham castle on the grand scale, CASTLE DROGO (Devon), and one pious restoration or re-creation, EILEAN DONAN, both begun before the war, were completed around 1930; and nothing like them has been done since. The sham castle, like the true one, has passed into history and become part of the national heritage.

OTHER SHAMS AND HYBRIDS

Layer Marney Tower (Essex) is a great martial gatehouse, erected as the entrance to a Tudor mansion that was never built. Tutbury (Staffordshire) combines medieval ruins with an 18th-century 'keep'. At Belvoir (Leicestershire) 19th-century Gothic, and at Brodick (Strathclyde) 'Scottish baronial', are superimposed on earlier remains. Two works by the celebrated 19th-century revivalist architect Anthony Salvin are Muncaster (Cumbria) and Peckforton (Cheshire). Castell Coch (South Glamorgan) is William Burges' brilliant re-creation of a 13th-century castle, built for the Marquis of Bute. New Scottish 'castles' include Robert Adam's Culzean (Strathclyde; 18th-century Gothic), Barry's Dunrobin (Highland; French château style), and Playfair's Floors (Borders; baronial).

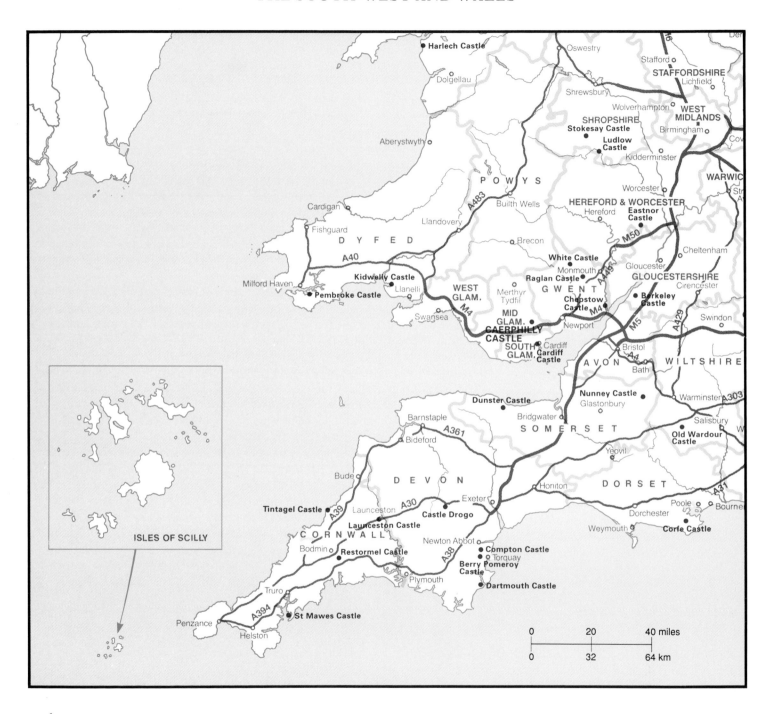

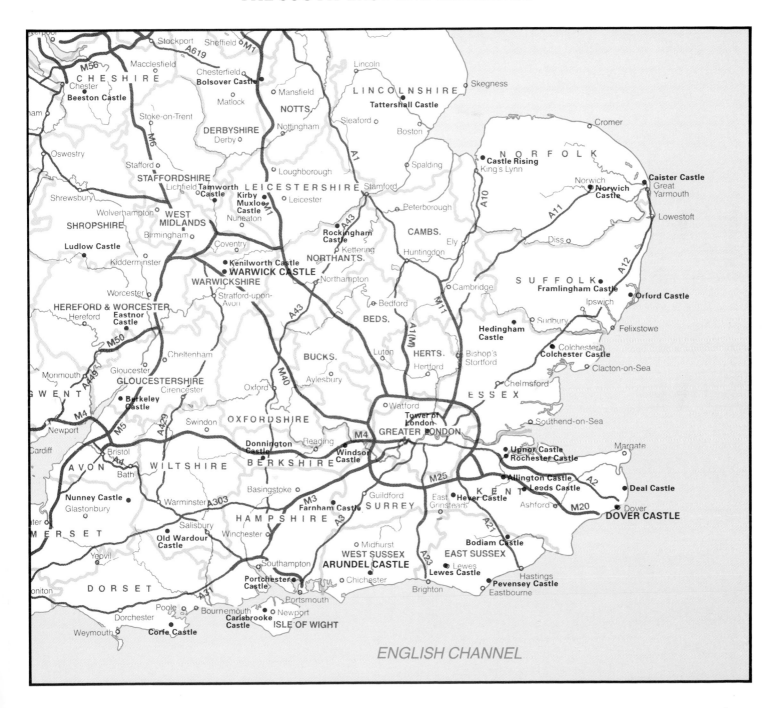

SCOTLAND

2
Gazetteer

ALLINGTON CASTLE KENT

Although much restored, Allington is an impressive-looking castle with many interesting features from the medieval and Tudor periods. An Allington Castle was one of many private fortresses pulled down by Henry II after he had crushed the rebellion of 1173–4, but the earliest parts of present-day Allington belong to a castle of the later courtyard type, with rectangular walls defended by a gatehouse and mural towers. This was built by Stephen de Penchester, who was granted a royal licence in 1281; his great hall and the formidable Solomon's Tower still stand.

Allington passed via the Cobhams to the Wyatts, whose fluctuating fortunes were in many ways typical of the Tudor period. Sir Henry Wyatt, having opposed Richard III, became *persona grata* with Richard's conqueror, Henry VII, and by 1492 was able to buy Allington. His son, Sir Thomas Wyatt, survived the shifts of Henry VIII's reign with only brief spells out of favour or in prison. But the next Sir Thomas made Allington the headquarters of a Kentish conspiracy prompted by Queen ('Bloody') Mary's unpopular plan to wed Philip II of Spain. Wyatt's bold march on London came close to overthrowing the established order – but, failing, cost him his life. After centuries of uneventful decline, Allington was finally restored from 1905.

2 miles (3 km) north-west of
Maidstone, on the A20 (map page 61)

◆

Left *The ruins of Corfe Castle in Dorset*

ALNWICK CASTLE NORTHUMBERLAND

Alnwick (pronounced 'Annick') was the most powerful stronghold of the greatest northern English lords: the Percy Earls of Northumberland. However, the de Vescis family was here first, and in 1095 put up a stone shell keep on the motte, situated centrally between two enclosures; the larger of these, the (western) outer bailey, faced the town, while the inner bailey lay behind the keep, to the east.

It was from the de Vescis' castle of Alnwick in 1174 that a sudden foray led to the capture of William the Lion, King of Scotland, a famous episode since it turned the Scottish invasion into a débâcle and forced William to recognize England's Henry II as his feudal overlord. But Scotland's dependence was short-lived, and a new cycle of wars during the 14th century gave the Percys their opportunity to rise and a pressing reason to strengthen Alnwick, which they bought from the Bishop of Durham in 1309. The first two Percy lords gave the castle most of its main features, while following the basic Norman layout. The keep was transformed by the addition of seven semicircular wall towers; a great hall linked it with a gatehouse on the south curtain, firmly separating the baileys; the curtain walls were strengthened with interval towers; and a twin-towered gatehouse and splendid barbican were built to protect the west wall of the outer bailey. All these have survived, despite the many alterations made at Alnwick over the centuries. The Percys' power fell away during the Tudor period, but their remote descendants as Dukes of Northumberland made the castle not only habitable but opulent.

In the 18th century it was refurbished in mock-Gothic style, and stone 'soldiers' were placed on the barbican.

Continued on page 68

Guided Tour

◆

ARUNDEL CASTLE WEST SUSSEX

In the 900 years since its foundation as a Conquest castle, Arundel has been severely damaged and extensively rebuilt, so that much of the present fabric dates from the 18th and 19th centuries. But as well as its attractions as the residence of England's premier duke, it does also preserve the unusual layout and certain essential features of the original fighting castle.

The 70 ft (21 m) motte with two baileys – one on either side – was put up by Roger de Montgomery after William the Conqueror had named him Earl of Arundel in 1067. The castle was intended to bar the way to any invader landing on the Sussex coast from the sea, which is visible on a clear day from the top of the stone shell keep that now stands on the mound. Most of this seems to have been the work of William d'Albini, who also built the great keep at CASTLE RISING (Norfolk). As the husband of Henry I's ex-queen, d'Albini entertained Henry's daughter Matilda at Arundel after she landed in England in 1139, and supported her claim to the throne in the ensuing civil war against King Stephen. A brief, unsuccessful siege of Arundel by Stephen was only the second in the castle's history, and the last during the medieval period. The d'Albinis

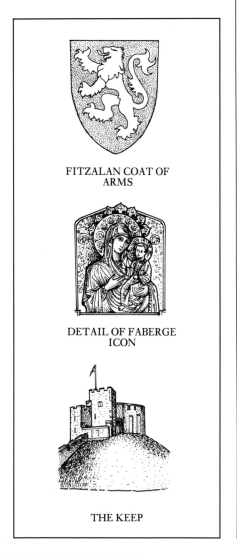

FITZALAN COAT OF ARMS

DETAIL OF FABERGE ICON

THE KEEP

remained in possession until 1243, when the male line became extinct and the castle and estate passed by marriage to the Fitzalans. In similar circumstances, the Howard Dukes of Norfolk inherited both castle and title in 1580; and they are still the incumbents of the castle. During the Civil War it was held for the King until 1643; then it was besieged, bombarded into surrender, and eventually slighted so thoroughly that it was uninhabitable until rebuilding began in the late 18th century.

The route up to the castle takes the visitor past the south and west fronts, which are splendidly medieval and martial in the best too-good-to-be-true Victorian fashion – remarkable examples of the scale on which 19th-century wealth was poured into the realization of baronial fantasies. By contrast, the castle is entered through the ruggedly foursquare flint and sandstone towers of the barbican, built in about 1295 by Richard Fitzalan and provided with two portcullises; the walls still carry the marks made by cannonballs during the siege of 1643. Beyond lies a still older gateway (*c.* 1100) and, above it, the rooms which Queen Matilda is traditionally said to have occupied.

The sturdy shell keep stands 30 ft (9 m) high, and in places its wall is 10 ft (3 m) thick. It is unusually richly decorated, with pilaster strips at intervals round the walls and Norman zigzags and scroll mouldings surrounding the former doorway (now blocked). Although the interior has long been gutted, some of the fireplaces are still visible, and there is a basement storeroom beneath the floor. The doorway is commanded by a tall, square tower which contained a well. A staircase

The south front of Arundel Castle, which has been home to the Dukes of Norfolk since 1580

leads up to the battlements, from which the views of the South Downs and the coast are truly spectacular.

The state and private apartments are laid out in three ranges around the lower bailey, now known as the Quadrangle. The interiors are mainly Victorian-medieval and of high quality, although the library remains as an example of the 11th Earl's less sober 18th-century 'Gothic', which his descendants disapproved of and largely swept away. As well as the enormous 'Baron's Hall' and other formal rooms for entertaining, there are smaller family apartments in the east wing. The contents of Arundel Castle reflect the varied history of the Howards as England's premier dukes, collectors, travellers, and Catholics steadfast in adversity – not only portraits, furniture, armour, ceremonial robes and *objets d'art*, but more eccentric items such as an 18th-century sleigh and bells carried off from Sevastopol after the Crimean War.

In the town, 9 miles (14.5 km) west of Worthing, on the A27 (map page 61)

The Percy stronghold of Alnwick Castle

Continued from page 65

(They may or may not have been based on medieval originals, formerly used, it is said, to suggest the presence of a large, watchful but remarkably sluggish garrison.) In the 19th century Alnwick was revamped again, and the large, square Prudoe Tower was added to the keep. The contents of Alnwick are as rich and varied as its fabric.

30 miles (48 km) north of Newcastle,
off the A1 (map page 62)

APPLEBY CASTLE   CUMBRIA

Appleby offers an entertaining range of experiences, for the castle stands at the heart of a Rare Breeds Survival Trust Centre and within the space of a few minutes the visitor can view the keep, Tamworth pigs, great hall, Bagot goats, Warwickshire Longhorns and various other delights. The site is a loop in the River Eden, and the castle itself stands at the far end of Appleby's spacious main street.

There was a motte-and-bailey castle here in the 11th century, but its only remains are the earthworks thrown up around it. At some undetermined point in the 12th century the motte was levelled, a square stone keep was raised on it, and the bailey was enclosed by a stone curtain wall. Only parts of the curtain survive, along with just one of the mural towers attached to it in the following century, while the

15th-century gatehouse is no more than an unrecognizable lump of masonry beside the entrance. But the four-storey keep, known as 'Caesar's Tower', stands to its full height, and all the floors and battlements are accessible. As usual, the entrance is at first-floor level, via a set of stone steps, although a separate outside doorway now leads into the ground-floor gift shop. The most curious, unexplained feature of the keep is that although there are windows on the lower floors, there are none just where one would expect to find them, safely beyond enemy reach on the top storey which was added in the 13th century.

On the other, east side of the bailey, the 17th-century domestic buildings incorporate much of the stonework of the medieval great hall. By the 1540s Appleby was a 'ruinous castle wherein the prisoners be kept', and Parliament made it still more ruinous by slighting it after the Civil War. Luckily Appleby was part of the far-flung Clifford estates, and the last of the line, the redoubtable Lady Anne Clifford, piously restored it during the 1650s along with other northern family castles such as SKIPTON (North Yorkshire), and Brough and Brougham (both in Cumbria).

In the town, 13 miles (21 km) south-east of Penrith, on the A66 (map page 62)

BAMBURGH CASTLE   NORTHUMBERLAND

Bamburgh Castle occupies a superb defensive site – a green, rocky headland standing out above the shore, with one side falling precipitously into the sea. Offering such obvious natural advantages, the headland was used as a stronghold from early times and the Anglo-Saxon king Ida of Bernicia is said to have fortified it in the 6th century. In the Norman period, in 1095, a castle at Bamburgh was besieged by William II (William Rufus), defying all his efforts to capture it until his threat to put out the eyes of its captive lord, Robert de Mowbray, Earl of Northumberland, induced the Earl's wife to surrender.

The present castle was begun in the 12th century, when King Stephen or possibly Henry II erected a keep on the top of the headland. This is the oldest and also the best preserved of the surviving medieval structures, although the original three storeys have been added to, and windows and widened loopholes give the building a rather unmilitary air. By about 1250 King John and his son, Henry III, had extended the castle so that it covered the entire headland, dividing it into three main areas enclosed by curtain walls with mural towers. These powerful defences subsequently proved their worth in border warfare, and later, during the Wars of the Roses, Henry VI and Queen Margaret chose Bamburgh as their headquarters when they attempted to reconquer England from the Yorkists. This was to spoil Bamburgh's impressive military record, for in 1463–4 it was besieged by the Earl of Warwick, who brought up two big guns that blasted a large hole in its walls, compelling an immediate surrender. Thus Bamburgh ended its career by becoming the first British castle to succumb to an artillery assault.

From the 18th century its rapid decay was halted by several benevolent owners, but it was the arms manufacturer Lord Armstrong who gave the castle its present form, carrying out extensive rebuilding between 1894 and 1903. As a result, Bamburgh is a curious, fascinating hybrid, combining stern medieval fact with comfortable modern fantasy.

16 miles (25.5 km) north of Alnwick, via
the A1 and B1341 (map page 62)

◆

BEAUMARIS CASTLE GWYNEDD

At first sight Beaumaris is a little disappointing, for although massive in extent it is disconcertingly low on the horizon. The reason for this is that the castle stands at sea-level, guarding the Menai Strait, and that, despite a 35-year building programme, the upper storeys and turrets of its great towers were never completed. Nevertheless, Beaumaris is deeply impressive in its sheer mass and scale, and above all in its splendidly regular design – one advantage of building on a featureless, flat terrain. It was the last of the great Edwardian fortresses of Wales, begun in 1295 immediately after the suppression of Madog's rebellion, when the inhabitants of the existing town of Llanfaes were uprooted to make way for a new English castle and town.

Beaumaris is a near-perfect example of a concentric castle. The very large, quadrangular inner ward is surrounded by a high curtain wall with boldly projecting drum towers at the corners, 'D'-plan towers in the middle of the east and west walls, and strong gatehouses dominating the other two sides; had it been built to its full height, the huge North Gatehouse would have dwarfed even its famous sibling at HARLECH (Gwynedd). The outer defences consist of a curtain wall with 12 towers and two gatehouses, and beyond it a moat which originally extended right round the castle and was supplied with tidal water; in the Middle Ages, sea-going vessels could reach the Castle Dock (next to the southern outer gate) and unload provisions directly into the interior. The southern route into the inner ward – through 'the Gate next the Sea', turning right into the barbican, and then passing through the South Gatehouse – gives a vivid sense of the hazards faced by attackers, with visible evidence of a lethal series of portcullises and murder holes.

Other interesting features include the wall-walks (the inner curtain walk boasting no less than eight neatly-designed sets of double latrines for the guards' use) and the long, atmospheric passages cut into the inner curtain.

5 miles (8 km) north-east of the Menai
Bridge, on the A545 (map page 62)

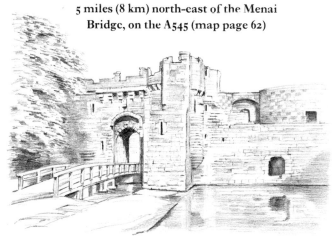

Beaumaris Castle, built by Edward I

BEESTON CASTLE   CHESHIRE

The ruins of Beeston bear melancholy witness to the triumph of time and change over even the most powerful fortress. This once formidable castle had natural advantages of a kind rare in England, since it stood some 500 ft (150 m) above the Cheshire plain on a rocky eminence with sheer cliff faces protecting its northern and western sides. It was built in the 1220s by Ranulf de Blundeville, Earl of Chester, who followed the latest military fashion by dispensing with a keep and relying on enclosing curtain walls defended by mural towers and a massive gatehouse. This layout survives on the heights at Beeston around the inner bailey or courtyard, although the remains of the walls and gatehouse of the sloping outer bailey are only fragmentary. The inner bailey is approached across a ditch cut into the rock, and the narrow, vaulted entrance in the middle of the south wall is dwarfed by the huge, squat, semicircular towers of a gatehouse that is truly massive, affording ample accommodation for the lord and his followers. There are two more semicircular towers in the south curtain wall, one on each side of the gatehouse, and a single rectangular tower stands close to the far end of the much shorter east curtain. To the north and west a plain curtain follows the cliff edge, since there was no point in constructing towers and directing flanking fire against enemy climbers, who – if spotted – would in any case be easy targets.

In the 1260s Beeston was one of Simon de Montfort's strongholds in his conflict with Henry III; and Richard II was popularly believed to have buried a great treasure here in 1399, just before his deposition and death. But Beeston Castle's disgrace and doom came during the Civil War, when the Parliamentarian garrison failed to guard the 'impregnable' north wall, which was scaled by a handful of Royalists who captured the castle. Later, by order of a victorious Parliament, Beeston was drastically slighted and never inhabited again.

12 miles (19 km) south-east of Chester,
via the A51 and A49 (map pages 61–2)

BERKELEY CASTLE   GLOUCESTERSHIRE

Castle and stately home, Berkeley has all the qualities that appeal to a romantic sense of the past: a venerable aspect, a pastoral tree-girt setting, and a long history that includes some thrilling and bloodcurdling moments. A single family has lived in the castle for over 800 years, and since the 14th century the concessions to the spirit of change have been relatively few and grudging; even the 35 ft (10.5 m) breach in the west wall, made by Parliamentary troops during the Civil War, remains unrepaired! Soon after the Conquest a timber castle was built here by William Fitz Osbern, Earl of Hereford. But the history of the present building begins in the 1150s, when Henry II rewarded Robert Fitzharding's services by making him lord of Berkeley, where his descendants still live. Fitzharding built a shell keep and enclosed the bailey with a stone curtain wall. The keep is, with FARNHAM (Surrey), one of the rare type built around the foot of the mound instead of its crest; and although the mound was subsequently removed, the floor is still much higher than ground level.

The most (in)famous episode in the castle's history occurred in 1327, when the deposed King Edward II was brought to Berkeley, where, when mistreatment failed to dispatch him, he was murdered, supposedly with a red-hot poker thrust 'through the secret place posterial'. Between 1340 and 1350 the castle was almost entirely rebuilt within its old walls, and it was then that the great hall and the chapel, with their splendid roofs, were put up. From this time, except for a three-day siege in the 17th-century Civil War, the history of the castle was fairly uneventful. However, the family's tenure was briefly interrupted when 'Waste-All' Berkeley parted with the castle to Henry VII in return for a marquisate, and possibly also to punish his heir for marrying a commoner. In 1549, when the last male Tudor, Edward VI, died, Berkeley Castle returned to the family, who have remained in possession ever since.

19 miles (30.5 km) south-west of Gloucester,
off the A38 (map pages 60–1)

Berkeley Castle, a great English stately home

BERRY POMEROY CASTLE DEVON

This is an enchanting ruin, standing high on a crag but hidden and romanticized by the dense woodland that surrounds it. Like the village nearby, it takes its name from the de la Pomeroi family, which 'came over with the Conqueror' and took root in Devon as prosperous gentry. However, there is no record of any building on the site before the earliest parts of the present castle were erected, and these are most commonly dated to the early 14th century. In its original form the castle probably followed a courtyard plan, from which the surviving elements are a gatehouse with two semi-hexagonal towers, the south curtain wall, and a 'U'-shaped corner tower (St Margaret's Tower) in the south-east angle.

The family lived at the castle until Sir Thomas Pomeroy was rash enough to join the great West Country rising of 1549 against the new Protestant regime whose figurehead as Lord Protector was Edward Seymour, Earl of Somerset. After the crushing of the rising it was the Seymours who bought the Pomeroy estates, including the castle. Although the Earl fell from power and was eventually executed, the Seymours remained a great family and soon afterwards, in the spirit of the Elizabethan age, decided to demonstrate the fact by building a splendid mansion on the north and east sides of the castle. It is the ruins of the mansion, added to the earliest remains, that make Berry Pomeroy such a fascinating hybrid, the battered mass of the gatehouse making an effective contrast with the east block, whose rows of large mullioned windows give an oddly skeletal look to the gutted, roofless walls. Although they remained in residence until about 1688, the Seymours never finished building their mansion. It is said to have been struck by lightning and destroyed by fire at some unspecified date towards the end of the 17th century.

1 mile (1.5 km) east of Totnes, off the A385
(map page 60)

◆

Left *The gatehouse of Berry Pomeroy Castle*

BLAIR CASTLE TAYSIDE

Time has rung many changes at Blair Castle. Its oldest part is named Cumming's Tower, after the John Comyn or Cumming who started building here in about 1269. He was an interloper who tried to establish himself at Blair while the rightful owner, the Earl of Atholl, was crusading in the Near East. Atholl earls and dukes have been in possession ever since, although the title passed from Strathbogies to Stewarts before being inherited in 1629 by the Murrays, who have held it ever since. In 1745, when Bonnie Prince Charlie landed in Scotland to claim the throne for the exiled Stuarts, the Murrays were divided in their allegiance. As a curious result, one of the Jacobite younger sons of the 1st Duke attempted to capture the family home, making it the last British castle to undergo a siege. As soon as the Jacobite rebellion was over, the 2nd Duke turned Blair into a Georgian mansion, taking down its parapets and turrets, remodelling the façade, and emphasizing the building's new civilian status by renaming it Atholl House. Internally his Rococo transformation of the castle has been allowed to survive, most memorably in the Picture Staircase that rises through two storeys to the splendid stucco ceiling, accompanied by 17th- and 18th-century Murray portraits ranging from beruffed sobriety to mock-Roman flamboyance. But outside, from 1869, the 7th Duke put the clock firmly back. Full of Victorian enthusiasm for the 'baronial' past, he gave Blair a new set of battlements and turrets (although he left the 18th-century sash windows incongruously in place), thereby completing its unusual evolution: from real fortress to sham castle.

1 mile (1.5 km) north-west of Blair Atholl,
off the A9 (map page 63)

◆

BODIAM CASTLE EAST SUSSEX

Bodiam is a great national treasure, splendidly preserved and a delight to contemplate across the wide, shining waters of the moat. It is the finest British example of a 14th-century courtyard castle, with an elegantly simple, near-symmetrical plan. Four ranges of two-storey buildings make up a quadrangle framing the courtyard. A tall drum tower stands at each corner of the quadrangle, and on two of the sides there is a square midpoint tower; the third and fourth (north and south) sides are dominated respectively by a substantial twin-towered gatehouse and a slighter postern tower.

Accommodation at Bodiam was not only plentiful but also luxurious, being equipped with the latest models of fire-places, chimney ducts and latrines. Although palatial enough for civilian use, the castle was actually built in the wake of a military emergency. In 1385 Sir Edward Dalyngrigge was given permission to 'strengthen and crenellate his manor house' in anticipation of a raid or invasion by the French, who had taken advantage of their temporary naval superior-ity to make a number of destructive descents on the English coast. The crisis soon passed, but in the meantime Dalyngrigge went far beyond his brief, putting up an entirely new castle.

Although considerations of self-glorification and creature comfort were evidently involved in its creation, Bodiam does seem to have been designed with an eye to possible military use. The causeway that now runs straight across the moat was formerly laid out with a right-angle turn to expose an attacker's flank, and this entire line of approach bristled with drawbridges, portcullises and other defences, of which only

Bodiam, a superb example of a 14th-century castle

the great gatehouse and part of a barbican remain. Moreover, the gatehouse carried gunports for cannon and could be sealed off to function as an independent unit if the rest of the castle fell or was taken over by internal dissidents. In the event, Bodiam's history was a peaceful one, and it even escaped slighting after the Civil War. But it was ruinous and abandoned until Lord Curzon took it over in 1917, lavishly restored it, and in 1925 presented it to the nation.

**12 miles (19 km) north of Hastings,
off the A229 (map page 61)**

BOLSOVER CASTLE DERBYSHIRE

A fascinating minor landmark in the history of taste, Bolsover is a 17th-century mansion with a martial air; and one part of it constitutes a very early example of a nostalgia-based genre with a remarkable future – the sham castle. The mansion was built for Sir Charles Cavendish on the site of the 12th-century castle belonging to William Peveril, which has vanished so completely that the only plausible explanation seems to be that the new Bolsover was literally superimposed on the old. The 'Keep' or 'Little Castle' was actually the first building put up here by Cavendish in about 1608; its architect was probably John Smythson, son of the more famous Robert. It is rectangular and battlemented, with square turrets at three corners and a large square staircase tower at the fourth; in traditional fashion it has a kitchen and other domestic offices in the semi-basement, a hall above it and two upper storeys of private rooms.

But if the building's military function was purely imagin-ary, it was certainly not a sham residence, being endowed with panelled and painted walls, ornate fireplaces and other features that have undergone careful restoration in recent years. Of the other buildings erected at Bolsover during the following 20 years or more, the terrace range, now roofless, is of particular interest. It has a huge long gallery and carries a wealth of elaborate and eccentric decoration, for example

The 'Little Castle' at Bolsover, viewed from the south

the pilasters half-way up the outside walls, which take the form of upward-pointing cannons!

6 miles (9.5 km) east of Chesterfield,
on the A632 (map pages 61–2)

BOLTON CASTLE   NORTH YORKSHIRE

Bolton is a grand, grim example of a northern courtyard castle, very different in atmosphere from a southern contemporary of the same type, such as BODIAM (East Sussex). In particular, the northern preference for rectangular towers and the absence of water defences meant that Bolton lacked two of the softening features that give BODIAM its charm. But despite its business-like appearance, the northern stronghold was constructed with space and comfort very much in mind. It consisted of a quadrangle of three-storey buildings surrounding a courtyard, with a five-storey tower at each corner. A smaller tower stood in the middle of each of the longer (north and south) walls. But there was no great gatehouse, only an arched passage driven through the buildings on the east side, close to the south-east tower. This arrangement allowed Bolton's lord to control the passage-way from the portcullis room adjacent to the tower, which housed his private quarters; these formed the nucleus of a small castle-within-the-castle, which could only be entered through a single ground-floor door.

Bolton Castle was built from about 1375 for Richard Scrope, who seems to have begun work well in advance of the licence to crenellate issued by Richard II in 1379. After an uneventful history, the castle served in 1568–9 as the first of the English prisons to hold Mary, Queen of Scots, after her flight into England. Although slighted by Parliament after the Civil War, Bolton is still in good condition, and in recent years it has been refurbished.

11 miles (17.5 km) south of Richmond,
via the A6108 and A684 (map page 62)

CAERLAVEROCK CASTLE
DUMFRIES AND GALLOWAY

Caerlaverock has the distinction of being the only tri-angular castle in Britain. In all other respects it was a conventional fortress, consisting of three high curtain walls with a massive, twin-towered gatehouse at the apex, on the northern, most vulnerable side, and a strong round tower at each of the other two angles; two sets of moats and earth ramparts made up the outer defences. It is not clear why the triangular plan was adopted, or even who built the castle. Caerlaverock stands guard over the Solway Firth, in a position that can be interpreted as either an obstacle to invaders or a bridgehead constructed by them; and since the castle dates from the 1290s and has many 'Edwardian' features, it may originally have been English-built. If so, it was soon lost to the Scots, for Edward I besieged and captured it in 1300. Twelve years later it was back in Scots hands and was being dismantled by Sir Eustace Maxwell as part of the anti-English 'scorched earth' policy pursued by Robert the Bruce. Although Caerlaverock nevertheless saw much action during subsequent hostilities, it was evidently in poor condition until the 15th century, when it was rebuilt and the gatehouse in particular was strengthened; a century or so later it was equipped with gunports. The Maxwells remained in occupation over these centuries, and in about 1634 Robert Maxwell, 1st Earl of Nithsdale, built a fine three-storey domestic block in Renaissance style; its walls are now the principal remains within the castle curtain. Six years later he conducted a gallant three-month defence against the Covenanters, as a result of which Caerlaverock was harshly slighted and abandoned.

12 miles (19 km) south-east of
Dumfries, on the B725 (map page 62)

CAERNARFON CASTLE   GWYNEDD

We can be almost certain that the regal, slightly exotic aspect of Caernarfon Castle is exactly what was intended by Edward I when he ordered Master James of

Caernarfon symbolized English domination of Wales

St George to begin building it in 1283. The result was a fortress-palace that deliberately recalled the Theodosian walls of Constantinople, the most famous city in medieval Christendom: reminiscent in its high curtain walls, in its polygonal towers (contrasting with the round towers used on all Edward's other castles), and in the distinctive bands of different coloured stone running round the exterior.

Evidently the King always intended Caernarfon to be the capital of the newly conquered principality, and he contrived to have a son, Edward, born there in 1284 and declared Prince of Wales. (He later, as Edward II, became one of England's unluckiest monarchs.)

Caernarfon Castle is roughly oblong in plan, narrowing slightly in the middle where a cross-wall once divided it into two wards or baileys. The shape of the outer, eastern ward was determined by the mound on which it stands; this was the site of a Norman motte-and-bailey castle erected in about 1090, during an earlier invasion from England. The more regularly laid out inner ward boasts one of the castle's most imposing features, the triple-turreted Eagle Tower, 120 ft (37 m) high. After ten years of hugely expensive building, work at Caernarfon stopped, although much was still to be done – and as a result, both the town and the castle were overwhelmed when Madog rebelled in 1294–5. After this blow to English prestige, work resumed in a second phase lasting from 1294 to 1330. Parts of the castle remained unfinished even then, but it nevertheless proved strong enough to withstand Owain Glyndŵr in 1403–4.

Centuries of decay followed, but a programme of restoration was encouraged by the decision to invest the Prince of Wales at Caernarfon in 1911. The ceremony was performed there again in 1969, when Prince Charles received the title. Caernarfon Castle is now a magnet for visitors to North Wales; among its attractions are a variety of excellent displays and exhibitions.

In the centre of Caernarfon, on the A487
(map page 62)

CAISTER CASTLE   NORFOLK

One of the earliest brick castles, Caister is a high, dramatic ruin with some unusual features and an interesting, well-documented history. Its nucleus was built on a conventional courtyard plan, but the west corner was occupied by a single tall round tower that must have dominated the castle even when all the other buildings were intact. Fortunately the tower and the adjacent west curtain wall are the most substantial survivals at Caister, their elegantly designed machicolations demonstrating that the castle was a showpiece. The tower still stands to a height of 90 ft (27·5 m), and looks even taller because of its slenderness; by a happy accident its stair turret has fared even better, so that it now rises some 8 ft (2·5 m) above the tower to create a nice sculpturesque effect.

Caister was built for Sir John Fastolf, a veteran of the French wars who had made a fortune in ransom-money; echoes of his slightly dubious reputation are heard in Shakespeare's *Henry VI* and in the name of the dramatist's most famous comic character, the fat, cowardly Falstaff. Work at Caister began in 1432 and went on into the 1440s; as we know from the accounts, the bricks were fired locally, but the stone for dressings was imported from France. As well as the main quadrangle, there was a large enclosure on each side of the castle, which was protected by exceptionally elaborate water defences.

Continued on page 81

77

Guided Tour

CAERPHILLY CASTLE
MID GLAMORGAN

Caerphilly is the classic British example of a concentric castle, vast in area and bristling with effective defences, among them a large artificial lake. The castle was begun in 1268 by the English Marcher lord Gilbert de Clare, and despite a drastic incursion by his enemy Llywelyn ap Gruffydd it was erected in the course of the 1270s and 1280s. The only substantial later work was a rebuilding of the great hall in the 1320s. In spite of this Caerphilly was soon abandoned, and as a result of its subsequent decay, what we now see owes a great deal to 19th- and 20th-century restorations.

The castle is entered across an outer moat and through the main eastern gatehouse (the first of three increasingly formidable entrances), which features a highly informative permanent exhibition. Stretching away on either side of it are the north and south dams, each with its own gatehouse at the far end. A second bridge crosses the inner moat to the central island, which constitutes the still-concentric heart of Caerphilly.

The outer curtain wall runs round the edge of the island, and although always lower than the inner curtain, is now disproportionately broken down. The towers of its gateway are substantial, but they are dwarfed by the mighty gatehouse to the inner ward, looming up directly behind them. The most powerful single element in the entire castle, this also happens to be the least original, since Gilbert de Clare simply copied the design from a gatehouse put up at Tonbridge in Kent by his own

father! Nevertheless, it was an early example of the gatehouse-as-keep, capable of functioning independently when the rest of the castle had been overthrown. Its three storeys and sizeable hall were probably the residence of the constable.

To right and left of the inner gatehouse

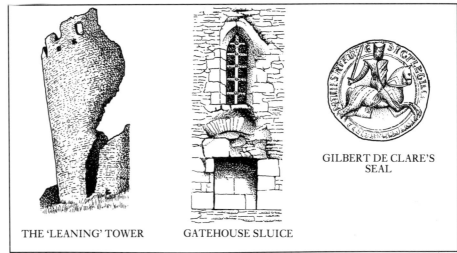

THE 'LEANING' TOWER   GATEHOUSE SLUICE

GILBERT DE CLARE'S SEAL

are the fallen north-east corner tower and the extraordinary south-east tower, whose 10-degree tilt outleans the Tower at Pisa. The split that caused it was non-military, probably resulting from subsidence. Inside the inner ward stands the great hall, which was extensively rebuilt in the 1320s for Hugh le Despenser, doomed favourite of the equally doomed Edward II. It was both spacious and well lit. The present roof is Victorian, but the medieval original represented something of a feat, spanning some 35 ft (10·5 m) without supporting aisles; the wall columns rise from stone corbels, each of which is carved into three heads, believed to represent the King and other notables. As the large, high, pointed windows indicate, the hall was for use on comfortably peaceful occasions.

Caerphilly, the largest castle in Wales and the first to be concentric

Beyond the great hall lie the remains of private apartments and the north-east tower, which is almost entirely a modern reconstruction; however, the north-west 'Lady's Tower' is authentic.

Beyond the inner and outer gatehouses, and across another bridge, is the featureless western island. To judge by its careful shaping and its corset of stone, it was an important outwork, although its exact function is not known. Across a final bridge from the western island are some earthworks dating from the 17th-century Civil War, which must have some connection with the castle; and these in turn stand within the site of a Roman fort. The western island has a further link with the castle via the north bank, a narrow strip of land that bypasses the central island and leads directly round to the main entrance.

In the centre of Caerphilly, on the A469 (map page 60)

Continued from page 77

An inventory of Sir John's possessions reveals just how comfortable a 15th-century castle could be, offering a large number of separate lodgings with their own fireplaces and lavatories, carpets and feather beds. Fastolf died childless in 1459, leaving his estate to his friend John Paston – another lucky accident, since the family correspondence (the famous 'Paston Letters') gives a vivid picture of the siege of 1469 in which 3000 men in the service of a greedy magnate, the Duke of Norfolk, seized Caister; the letters reveal that the defenders made good use of the castle's gunports until the powder ran out. The Pastons recovered Caister six years later and lived there until 1599, when it was abandoned.

2 miles (3 km) west of Caister-on-Sea, on the A1064 (map page 61)

◆

CARDIFF CASTLE   SOUTH GLAMORGAN

Standing just across the road from the precincts and arcades of the city centre, Cardiff Castle offers an entertainingly assorted selection of historical pleasures. From the 1st century AD the Romans were here, building and rebuilding, and parts of their fort's wall have survived, now helpfully demarcated by a red stone outline. The Norman remains are far more substantial – the mound raised in the north-west corner of the Roman fort in 1191 by Robert Fitz Hamon, and the 12th-century, 12-sided shell keep that replaced the earlier structure.

Despite its compactness, this is a rather bleak, tough little fortress, fascinatingly different in mood from the range of buildings and towers in the south-west corner. These, although incorporating medieval fabric, are essentially a creation of high-minded Victorian medievalism; and the same is true of their extraordinary and literally fantastic interiors, which were conceived by the 3rd Marquis of Bute, designed by William Burges, and carried out under his direction by teams of artists and craftsmen.

Visitors go up into a covered parapet walk, past shuttered

Left The west side of Cardiff Castle

embrasures commanding the traffic, and enter a medieval never-never land of incredible opulence, meticulous craftsmanship and eccentric ingenuity, dense with carving, painting and gilding, tiles, metalwork, stained glass, marquetry and marble . . . . Among the high points of the guided tour are the Earl's bachelor quarters in the Clock Tower, replete with elaborate, multi-layered symbolism on the theme of time, the claustrophobic honeycombed Arab Room, the vast Banqueting Hall, and the delightful Roof Garden. Bute's castle is a folly, but folly on a grand and glorious scale.

In the centre of Cardiff, on the A470 (map page 60)

◆

CARISBROOKE CASTLE   ISLE OF WIGHT

Time has made of Carisbrooke a lush and lovely place, attractive to visitors of all ages. But for an exceptionally long period the castle was a carefully maintained military installation, designed to prevent any attacker from taking over the Isle of Wight and using it as a base from which to invade the mainland. Constantly repaired and brought up to date, Carisbrooke's principal features are mostly hybrids, as alert visitors will notice at once when they pass into the castle beneath the gunports and through the Elizabethan arch of the medieval gatehouse. Saxon remains

Carisbrooke, strategically located on the Isle of Wight

have been discovered in the earthworks that surround Carisbrooke, and a timber motte-and-bailey castle was erected after the Conquest by William Fitz Osbern. It was replaced early in the 12th century by the present shell keep, which stands in the north-east corner of the curtain wall put up at about the same time. The origins of the gatehouse lie in the 13th century, and this is also true of most of the domestic buildings, thanks to the energetic efforts of Isabel de Fortibus (d. 1295), the widow of one of the lords of the Isle, who is said to have effectively re-created the castle.

The importance of Carisbrooke was emphasized during the Hundred Years War, and in 1377 it was besieged without success by French raiders. In 1588 the castle was strengthened against a possible landing by the Spanish Armada which never materialized. Fear of Spain prompted further work in 1597–1600, when a famous Italian engineer, Gianibelli, constructed the outer line of defences; its corners are arrowhead bastions – out-thrusting platforms from which the defenders could direct raking fire at enemies assaulting the curtain wall. Another Tudor addition is the well-house, built around a well sunk as long ago as 1150; this is one of the castle's most popular features, thanks to the donkeys who work the great oak windlass. The Governor's lodgings held prisoner King Charles I, who left them only to return to London and meet his doom.

On the south-west outskirts of
Newport, off the B3323 (map page 61)

Castle Drogo devon

Castles continue to haunt the British imagination, but it comes as a surprise to find imitations being built as late as the second and third decades of the 20th century. Yet this was literally the case at Castle Drogo, begun in 1910 and not completed until 1930. It was the brainchild of Julius Drewe, founder of the Home and Colonial Stores, who chose a site near the village of Drewsteignton, in an area once dominated by the Drus or Drogos, whom he supposed to have been his Norman baronial forebears. The architect was

Sir Edwin Lutyens, already at the head of his profession and soon to take up an even more monumental project, the designing of an imperial capital, New Delhi, for British India.

Castle Drogo was built of granite (the local stone) and also stands on granite – a bluff some 1000 ft (300 m) above the gorge of the River Teign, affording lovely views of Dartmoor. Monotony is avoided by skilful recessing on the façade of this huge battlemented mansion, although its austere, clean-edged plainness is not to all tastes. Inside as well as out, the rather spartan designs reflect an outlook that seems to have been based on the bareness of long-ago-gutted castles rather than the colours and patterns that we know represented their original owners' tastes. Drogo, the last British castle built on the grand scale, is basically an Edwardian fantasy-fortress; and so it is not inappropriate that visitors should now be invited to collect bats, balls and hoops, and play croquet on the lawn.

12 miles (19 km) west of Exeter, via the
A30 and A382 (map page 60)

Castle Rising norfolk

The massive 12th-century keep at Castle Rising stands in virtually solitary grandeur on its oval ringwork, with only the broken remains of a bridge and gatehouse in front of it. The ringwork is set in a wider rectangular earthwork that is well worth a second look, since it is unusually distinct and well preserved, possibly going back to Roman or even earlier times. However, little is known about the site until after the Norman Conquest, when King William confiscated it from the Saxon Archbishop of Canterbury, Stigand, and gave it to his half-brother, Odo, Bishop of Bayeux. After Odo forfeited it by rebelling, it passed to William d'Albini or d'Aubigny, whose son built the keep of Castle Rising in about 1140; he may well have been celebrating by building in stone, as the Normans were wont to do, since his marriage in 1138 to Henry I's widow, Queen Adelaide, had made d'Albini one of the most powerful men in the kingdom.

The keep at Castle Rising, built in about 1140

The keep is certainly imposing – not in height (about 55 ft, or 17 m, now that it lacks parapet and roof) but in extent (78 × 68 ft, or 23 × 20 m), affording ample room for provisions, services and spacious living in its two storeys. Access to the hall on the first floor was provided by an unusually well-preserved forebuilding with the remains of elegant decorative arcading, a particularly fine staircase and a vaulted vestibule. These prepared the visitor for a now vanished luxury and sophistication that are hard to imagine in the present bare, roofless, floorless keep, although the chapel, gallery, three surviving turrets and other features are of considerable interest. Castle Rising had a fairly uneventful history. It eventually passed to the Crown, and after her fall from power Edward II's widow, Queen Isabella, lived here from 1331 to 1351. Left to decay from early in the 15th century, Castle Rising finally passed to the Howards in 1544, and it remains Howard property, although it is administered by English Heritage.

6 miles (9.5 km) north of King's Lynn,
off the A149 (map page 61)

CAWDOR CASTLE HIGHLAND

This is an attractive castle whose rambling aggregation of buildings reveals that much has been added to it over the generations. But at its heart stands a five-storey medieval tower house, still reached by crossing a drawbridge over the ditch and passing through an entrance guarded by the traditional Scottish yett, or iron gate. Below its later crenellations, machicolations and cone-capped bartizans (projecting corner turrets), the tower is a plain, sturdy rectangle, said to date back to the late 14th century; the original first-floor entrance, reached by wooden stairs that could be moved at moments of peril, can still be seen on its east face.

The ground floor houses the dead stump of the hawthorn tree which, according to a famous legend, determined the site of the castle. The legend relates that the thane was instructed in a vision to load a donkey with his treasures, allow it to wander freely, and watch until it came to a group of three hawthorns; it would lie beneath the third, and the thane should – and evidently did – build on that spot!

Improvements and extensions were begun by the 6th Cawdor, or Calder, thane who secured a royal licence to crenellate in 1454. The castle passed to the Campbells after Muriel, the Cawdor heiress, was abducted in 1499 and married to Sir John Campbell. With the arrival of more peaceful times, ranges of buildings and courtyards were put up round the tower, notably by Sir Hugh Campbell during the late 17th century, and the Campbell earls still hold the castle.

4 miles (6.5 km) south-west of Nairn,
on the B9090 (map page 63)

CHEPSTOW CASTLE GWENT

A ruinous but magnificent procession of walls, towers and enclosures, Chepstow Castle marches from east to west down a narrow cliff top above the River Wye. Protected by steep inclines to north and south, it was well placed to control the vital river-crossing on the main route from England into South Wales; and its strategic importance led to generations of building activity that now make its layout seem, at first sight, rather mystifying.

The nucleus of the castle is a rectangular hall-keep built by William the Conqueror's trusted lieutenant William Fitz Osbern, before his death in 1071. He built in stone (making Chepstow arguably the earliest stone castle in Britain), which was also used for the curtain walls of the two baileys, one on each side of the keep.

The first significant new work was motivated by a desire to strengthen the castle's vulnerable east end. An outstanding soldier-statesman, William Marshal, became lord of Chepstow in 1189 and put up a new curtain wall along the east end of the bailey, incorporating two strong round towers – a very early British example of this new defensive scheme. Marshal's sons raised a barbican at the west end and added a third bailey on the east; and in accordance with the military wisdom of *their* day, they strongpointed the entrance with a twin-towered gatehouse. This completed the basic

The ruins of Chepstow Castle, sited above the River Wye

five-part layout of the castle (barbican, upper bailey, keep, middle bailey, lower bailey) as it now exists; the barbican that originally defended the outer gatehouse has vanished.

There were further additions in the last quarter of the 14th century by Roger Bigod, Earl of Norfolk, notably a palatial set of domestic apartments on the river side of the lower bailey and a great tower on its south-east corner intended for Bigod's own private use; it is now known as Marten's Tower, after a 17th-century political prisoner. Ironically, conflicts of arms largely passed Chepstow by until the Civil War, when it was twice besieged and captured, and even underwent some limited rebuilding before being left quietly to decay.

15 miles (24 km) east of Newport, on
the A48 (map page 60)

---◆---

CHIRK CASTLE CLWYD

Chirk is a historic castle that has been thoroughly domesticated over the centuries. It is entered by splendid 18th-century wrought-iron gates, is surrounded by parkland with a lake, and boasts a noble formal garden beside its east wing. Although the house itself is large and

a little dour, its military pretensions are modified by its setting, and by the many windows which replaced arrow-slits.

Yet Chirk originated as a Marcher castle, designed to hold down the conquered Welsh. It belonged to the second generation of 'Edwardian' fortresses, being built after 1282 on confiscated Welsh land for Roger Mortimer, one of King Edward's companions in arms. But it was never finished according to plan, perhaps because Welsh resistance appeared to have been broken. It was obviously intended to be a typical rectangular castle, with strong round corner towers and semicircular towers midway along each wall. But at Chirk the east and west curtains are truncated, ending just below the interval towers, and a plain south range, lacking the expected corner towers and massive gatehouse, seals the quadrangle. An equally curious feature is the unmilitary lowness of Chirk's towers, which rise to the same height as the curtain wall, giving the castle its distinctively earthbound quality.

In 1598 Chirk was bought by Sir Thomas Myddleton, merchant and sometime Lord Mayor of London, whose descendants still live in the castle. During the Civil War his son, another Thomas, found himself obliged to besiege his own castle on behalf of Parliament; but failed to take it. Later, in 1659, as a convert to Royalism, he tried with equal lack of success to hold Chirk for the King. However, a year later the newly installed Charles II rewarded him suitably, and Myddleton was able to repair the damage done at Chirk and begin its expansion and embellishment. Now, with its 17th-century long gallery, Adam-style state rooms, Victorian Gothic entrance hall and elegant furnishings, the former border fortress is a sumptuous stately home.

8 miles (13 km) north of Oswestry, off
the A483 (map page 62)

---◆---

CLIFFORD'S TOWER NORTH YORKSHIRE

Medieval York was the 'capital' of northern England, but there was no stone castle in the city until a surprisingly late date. After the Conquest, in order to control this important and hostile area King William built timber towers on two separate mottes, one on each side of the River Ouse; but in 1069 the citizens burned them down during the great rebellion that led to William's infamous 'harrying' (laying waste) of the North. A new timber tower was erected on one of the mottes, but it was burned down during a pogrom in 1190, along with the Jews who had taken refuge inside it. Rebuilt and blown down again by a gale, it was finally replaced by a stone keep in the mid 13th century. The bailey was enclosed by a stone wall furnished with towers and gate-houses, but of these only a stretch of wall and two towers survive at the southern end of the site.

Although a ruin, the keep is both visually impressive and very interesting because of its four-lobed or quatrefoil plan, virtually unique in England; the exterior consisted of four great tower-like curves, symmetrically arranged, with a narrow entrance block squeezed between two of the curves. The castle at York sprang into importance in the 14th century, when York became the headquarters of the English effort to conquer Scotland. The name of the tower only dates from the 17th century, although it was suggested by the fate of a member of the baronial opposition to Edward II, Lord Robert Clifford, whose body was hung in chains from the tower in 1322, when the King's party was temporarily in the ascendant. Within a few years the tower was being neglected, and its story was one of slow deterioration until the Civil War, when it was held for the King and suffered a heavy bombardment. Some repairs were done after the Restoration of 1660 (hence the Royal and Clifford Arms on the entrance block), but following a fire in 1684 the tower was finally abandoned.

In the centre of York, off the A19
(map page 62)

COLCHESTER CASTLE   ESSEX

Colchester Castle was one of the earliest of the great stone keeps built in England by the Normans. Dating from the 1080s, it is a near contemporary of the White Tower, the keep at the heart of the so-called TOWER OF LONDON (which is actually a concentric castle with many towers). Although rather less glamorous externally, Colchester has many points of resemblance to the White Tower, one of the most distinctive being that a chapel apse protrudes from the south-east corner of each castle; this suggests that Gundulf, Bishop of Rochester, who was responsible for the White Tower, also put up Colchester Castle.

The site had an ancient British and Roman history, and in characteristic fashion the Normans used the remains of the temple dedicated to the Emperor Claudius as the foundations for their keep. Perhaps inspired by the size of the temple, they constructed a huge keep, some 110×152 ft (33.5×46 m), which was not only bigger than the White Tower but bigger than any keep in Europe. It seems to have stood about 90 ft (27 m) high, although the outline of battlements still visible within the wall on the outside suggests that it was originally intended to be lower – or that, while still incomplete, it was prepared for action in an emergency such as a threatened Danish invasion.

Colchester belonged to the king's stewards, and later to the Crown itself. Despite its massiveness, its defensive record was unimpressive: it was surrendered twice – once to the French – during the wars at the end of King John's reign. The entire town of Colchester was held for Charles I in a gruelling siege from June to August 1648, but the castle surprisingly suffered little in the subsequent demolitions. However, only a few years afterwards an enterprising building contractor bought the keep and demolished the upper stages before deciding in the end that the job was too much for him.

Finally, in this century the castle passed into public care and now houses an excellent museum of British and Roman antiquities.

In the town, 18 miles (29 km)
south-west of Ipswich, on the A12
(map page 61)

The massive Norman keep of Colchester Castle, built in the 1080s

COMPTON CASTLE   DEVON

Compton is not a true castle but a fortified manor house with a curtain wall forming a courtyard; but it is redolent of the past and visually very exciting. Although its origins date back to the 14th century, the first serious defences seem to have been put up in the mid 15th century, prompted by the effectiveness of earlier French raids on the Devon coast. The third phase of building began in 1520, and it was at this time that Compton's superb façade was completed – an extraordinarily picturesque array of battlements, buttresses, archways and recesses in which an impression of clutter is avoided thanks to the disciplining influence of the hard, long verticals.

It would almost – but not quite – be true to say that there have always been Gilberts here; the most famous was the explorer Sir Humphrey Gilbert, who in 1583 claimed Newfoundland for the Crown (making it the first English colony), but perished at sea soon afterwards. Within a few years of his death, legend has it, Spanish prisoners from the Armada were set to work in the gardens at Compton. By 1800 the house was in poor condition and was sold; but in storybook fashion it was bought back into the family in this century by Commander Walter Gilbert, who restored it. The National Trust took it over in 1951, but Gilberts still live on the premises. Visitors are shown selected parts of the interior including the great hall (a modern restoration) and the 15th-century solar (withdrawing room) and chapel.

4 miles (6.5 km) south-west of Torquay,
via the A380 and A3022 (map page 60)

◆

CONISBROUGH CASTLE   SOUTH YORKSHIRE

Conisbrough must have seemed a bold experiment when it was first built, and it still makes a slightly eccentric impression. At its heart is a round keep, representing the most advanced late 12th-century military thinking; but the advantages of its shape were neutralized in a curious fashion by surrounding it with six massive buttresses which must have severely restricted the defenders' field of vision. Since the buttresses were solid stone all the way through, they did not even provide extra accommodation, except for one end of a small chapel which penetrated into a buttress. This seeming obsession with mass and stability appeared again, more justifiably, in the massive battered reinforcement of the keep's base. Military sophistication is also evident in the surviving sections of the curtain wall that formerly enclosed the bailey. Built soon after the keep, this was strengthened with projecting round interval towers which rose above the level of the wall-walks – possibly the earliest English example of round towers employed in this fashion.

Conisbrough figures in *Ivanhoe*, a famous historical novel by Sir Walter Scott – who, however, mistakenly took it for a Saxon castle. In fact, even the earthworks and first timber defences were probably erected by a Norman, William de Warenne, Earl of Surrey. The transition to stone in the 1180s was begun by Hamelin Plantagenet, Henry II's illegitimate half-brother, who married the Warenne heiress. If Conisbrough was built to advertise Hamelin's new wealth and power, this would explain the castle's advanced, perhaps only half-understood, design, as well as the installation of all the latest conveniences, including hooded fireplaces, in the four-storey keep. The first-floor entrance is now reached by a modern set of steps; stone stairs in the thickness of the wall lead to other levels, but the upper floors have

Compton Castle, a 14th-century fortified manor house

disappeared. Outside the keep, only sets of foundations signal the presence of other domestic buildings in the bailey. Decayed by Tudor times but untroubled by the Civil War, Conisbrough has survived as the 'rude yet stately building' that fired Scott's imagination.

4½ miles (7 km) south-west of
Doncaster, on the A630 (map page 62)

CONWY CASTLE GWYNEDD

Despite the loftiness of its walls and its eight round towers, Conwy has a close-massed, forbidding air that brings home to the visitor its role as a colonial outpost, at once oppressive and potentially beleaguered. The castle and town were begun in March 1283 on the orders of Edward I, whose troops were still engaged in crushing Welsh resistance further to the south. The work was carried out at great speed – much faster than the contemporary undertakings at CAERNARFON and HARLECH (both in Gwynedd) – and was effectively completed by the autumn of 1287.

Unlike that of the typically spacious and regular Edwardian castle, Conwy's plan comprises an elongated east–west rectangle with a pronounced bow-shaped bulge on part of its south side; the shape was dictated by the contours of the rock on which the castle stands. A cross-wall divides Conwy into inner (eastern) and outer (western) wards, each able to function independently in an emergency.

The larger outer ward is entered from the town via a barbican, although a winding path has replaced the stepped ramp and drawbridge that were once the only means of approaching it. The great hall, curving around the long south side of the ward, is the most impressive of the buildings still standing inside the castle. Nothing else remains in the outer ward, although it must once have been a crowded place, accommodating the garrison's quarters, the stables and the kitchens. The inner ward housed the royal apartments, including the King's Hall (the shell of which survives), and each of its four corner towers is dignified with a single neat round turret rising above it. A now-vanished water gate gave the inhabitants of the inner ward a lifeline to the sea via the east barbican.

Although King Edward himself was briefly besieged in Conwy early in 1295 during Madog's rebellion, the subsequent history of the castle was uneventful. As much of an attraction as the castle itself are the well-preserved walls of the adjoining town, with its three gates and 21 towers.

In the town, 4 miles (6.5 km) south of
Llandudno, on the A55 (map page 62)

CORFE CASTLE DORSET

Once said to be the strongest castle in the realm, Corfe is now a thorough ruin – but a spectacular one, with the remains of the keep standing up against the sky like broken blades. Its very success was its undoing, causing it to become the most savagely mauled of all the 'ruins that Cromwell knocked about a bit', and consequently it is not easy for visitors to orient themselves among the extensive remains. Corfe Castle was built on a hillock commanding a gap in the long ridge of the Purbeck Hills. A royal residence stood here in Saxon times, and the murder of King Edward in AD 978 is recalled by the name of the twin-towered 'Martyr's Gate' into the inner bailey. After the Conquest a curtain wall was raised on the summit, followed early in the 12th century by a rectangular keep. In the 13th century the castle reached it apogee. It was King John's favourite, and he spent £1400 on it, creating a new triangular west bailey and building an unfortified house, the 'Gloriette', within the inner bailey, just to the east of the keep; it consisted of a continuous range around a courtyard, including a hall, chapel and service areas. Corfe Castle was associated with many events of John's troubled reign, notably the supposed murder by starvation of 22 knights who supported his rival for the throne. Most of the remaining building at Corfe was done by John's son, Henry III, who created the large, long outer bailey running down the slope to the south, and by Edward I, who completed his father's work by putting up the twin-towered outer bailey gatehouse. Corfe remained a royal castle until 1572, when Elizabeth I gave it to Sir Christopher Hatton. It later passed to Sir John Bankes, whose intrepid wife held it for the King against a powerful besieging force for much of the Civil War. A few days after it was captured, Parliament decreed that it was 'to be demolished forthwith' – a harsh sentence that was carried out in deplorably dutiful fashion.

6 miles (9.5 km) south-west of Wareham,
on the A351 (map pages 60–1)

CRAIGIEVAR CASTLE   GRAMPIAN

Almost every writer calls Craigievar a fairy-tale castle, and the adjective can hardly be avoided, despite the fact that it belongs not to an imaginary chivalric age but to the Scots 17th century. It is a late example of an 'L'-plan tower house, made more compact by the addition of a square tower in the re-entrant (inner) angle of the building. As usual, the plain lower storeys blossom into an elegant spray of cone-topped turrets and gables, which are here variegated further by two little cupolas and a classical parapet at the top of the tower; these features, emphasized by Craigievar's soft-toned walls and beautifully judged proportions, make the castle an outstanding work of architecture.

Craigievar was begun early in the 17th century by John Mortimer, but most of the building was done between 1610 and 1626 by the neighbouring laird who bought the estate: William Forbes, known as 'Danzig Willie' on account of the fortune he had made in the Baltic trade. Forbes and his successors also used their wealth to create fine interiors including a vaulted great hall with a riotously-decorated moulded plasterwork ceiling, carved screens, a minstrel gallery, and a huge fireplace with a stucco panel above it exhibiting the Royal Arms.

Although built at a time of peace (after the union of the Scottish and English crowns in 1603), Craigievar was designed with an eye to defence: the only way into the castle was by a single door in the tower, and it was enclosed by a curtain wall, most of which has now vanished. Descend-

ants of the Forbes family occupied Craigievar until 1963, when it was purchased for the National Trust for Scotland.

26 miles (42 km) west of Aberdeen, via
the A944 and A980 (map page 63)

CRATHES CASTLE   GRAMPIAN

Crathes is a fine example of the traditional Scottish tower house, plain and fortress-like below (except for a large window inserted at first-floor level during the Victorian period) but becoming increasingly elaborate and fanciful as it rises and tapers. Built of granite on the common 'L'-plan, the tower was the 16th-century stronghold of the ancient Burnett family of Leys, whose part in the struggle for Scottish independence is commemorated by the Horn of Leys in the hall, said to have been the gift of Robert the Bruce.

Crathes was built by several generations of Burnetts between 1553 and 1596, eventually comprising four storeys and an attic. It rises to an irregular but fascinating skyline, replete with gables, angle and stair turrets, gargoyles and similar features. Inside, the hall stands on the first floor, above the kitchen and cellars; then come the bedrooms, and finally, on the top floor, the oak-panelled long gallery. Many of the ceilings at Crathes are painted with lively, colourful and charmingly naïve figures dating from about 1602.

Additional accommodation is provided by a wing attached to the tower – a plain two-storey building which is actually a restoration, carried out after a fire in 1966 destroyed the obtrusively enlarged 'Queen Anne' wing built in the 18th century. Later Burnetts created the pleasant gardens at Crathes early in this century, and there were members of the family living in the castle down to 1966.

15 miles (24 km) west of Aberdeen, on
the A93 (map page 63)

Right *Craigievar – a masterpiece of Scottish architecture*

Dartmouth Castle guards the entrance to the Dart estuary

DARTMOUTH CASTLE   DEVON

Dartmouth Castle is, to say the least, unusual in appearance, since it consists of just two adjacent towers, one of them rectangular and the other round. Standing on a steep hillside that rises above the estuary of the River Dart, this structure was intended from the first to serve as an artillery fort, twinned with Kingswear Castle on the other bank to control the approach to Dartmouth harbour from the sea. Begun in 1481, the castle was built by Dartmouth Corporation with royal (Yorkist) funds against a possible French landing in support of the Lancastrian Henry Tudor (later Henry VII).

It was among the earliest British fortifications to be built specifically for artillery, and was even more advanced in the way its weaponry was emplaced. The main battery was situated on the ground floor of the rectangular tower, where seven gunports were cut out just above the water line; their advanced feature was that each was splayed internally, so that a cannon could be swivelled rapidly from side to side, attaining a much wider field of fire than hitherto without making the gunport wider and more vulnerable at the front. A chain could be strung across the estuary to impede the enemy, and this too was controlled from the rectangular tower in conjunction with Kingswear Castle. Musketeers

originally occupied the ground floor of the round tower, but the advantages of guns and gunports were so apparent that both were soon installed.

Dartmouth Castle changed hands twice during the 17th-century English Civil War, but it was too obviously valuable to be slighted, and remained in service until recent times.

1 mile (1.5 km) south-east of
Dartmouth, on the B3205
(map page 60)

DEAL CASTLE   KENT

Deal Castle was the first of the three castles built on Henry VIII's orders to command the Downs, a crucially important anchorage between the coast of Kent and the Goodwin Sands. Except for the battlements (added in 1732), its appearance has remained practically unchanged since 1539–40, when its construction was hurried through in response to the threat of an invasion from the Continent. Despite this haste, the work was splendidly executed in Caen stone plundered from a suppressed friary, and the design cunningly united Renaissance symmetry with strict attention to military function.

The plan of Deal is a double cloverleaf or set of variations on the circle and arc. The central round tower is enclosed by six adjacent bastions, and these in turn are protected by an outer ring of six much larger bastions down in the moat. Consequently, every approach was abundantly covered by the fort's 145 openings for cannon and handguns, which could be trained on an enemy from no less than five different tiers. And thanks to skilfully placed staircases, the garrison (usually, at Deal, an officer and 24 men) could make effective use of the firepower at its disposal. However, traditional techniques were not entirely abandoned, and an attacker who reached the main entrance might still find himself shot, stunned or scalded through the murder holes above the doorway. After a century of alarms, Deal Castle was finally put to the test in 1648, during the second Civil War between Charles I and Parliament; although never intended to withstand attack by land, it held out for the King until the Royalist cause was obviously lost.

In the town, 8 miles (13 km) north-east
of Dover, on the A258 (map page 61)

DONNINGTON CASTLE   BERKSHIRE

The gatehouse at Donnington stands proud and high, effectively the only survivor of an epic 17th-century siege. It was built in about 1386 for Sir Richard Abberbury, who added it to a fortified manor house of the courtyard type, with four round corner towers and a wall tower midway along two of the sides. The gatehouse projected from the third, east side, and consisted of a three-storey rectangular block flanked by round towers rising a storey higher. It was unmistakably designed to impress, with its high, tube-like towers; the projecting ribs of string coursing that ring the towers and run along the wall faces, marking off the different storeys; the mouldings round the door to the entrance passage; and the fine vaulted entrance passage itself. By 1586, when the antiquarian William Camden described it in his book *Britannia*, Donnington was a pleasant, many-windowed residence whose military future seemed non-existent. But when the Civil War came, the castle was held for the King by the intrepid Colonel John Boys and besieged, bombarded, relieved and reinvested for almost two years from 1644 to 1646. However, the obstacle to the Parliamentary army was not the castle but the vast, elaborate earthworks thrown up round Donnington according to the latest military principles. Thanks to these the Royalists held out; but by the time the garrison surrendered on terms and marched out with the honours of war, the besiegers' cannon had pounded most of the castle into rubble – all but the gatehouse, which miraculously remained upright.

1 mile (1.5 km) north of Newbury, on
the B4494 (map page 61)

DOUNE CASTLE   CENTRAL

Doune is a rugged monument to the power of Robert Stewart, 1st Duke of Albany, who built the castle at a strategic point on the main route into the Highlands from Edinburgh. A younger son of King Robert II, Albany dominated Scottish affairs for 30 turbulent years, governing the country in the name of his incapable older brother and, later, of James I, who was kidnapped and held captive by the English for 17 years.

The principal features of Albany's castle are two tall, strong, gabled towers which are connected by a lower range of buildings. The five-storey larger tower served as the incumbent's residence, with a vaulted great hall on the first floor. It was also the castle's gatehouse, giving the Duke and his successors direct control over the raising and lowering of the portcullis – an important consideration at a time when allegiances were extremely uncertain. For similar reasons, the Duke's tower was designed as an entirely independent unit, with its own well. The only entrance was up a set of steps from the courtyard, and although adjacent to the great hall, the retainers' hall was sealed off from it. (The present doorway between the two is a modern insertion.)

Albany died in 1420, and in 1425 the arrest and execution of his son probably brought building on the site to a premature end, so that the rest of the castle courtyard is only enclosed by a simple curtain wall. Doune became Crown property until the late 16th century, when it passed to the Stewart Earls of Moray. Despite an uneventful history it fell into ruins during the late 18th century, but it was meticulously restored during the 1880s by the 14th Earl.

9 miles (14.5 km) north-west of Stirling,
on the A84 (map page 63)

DRUM CASTLE   GRAMPIAN

Drum Castle is unusual in that its owner-improvers left its medieval defensive tower untouched, choosing to add to it rather than 'modernize' it. As a result, the castle somewhat incongruously unites a sturdy 13th-century

Continued on page 96

Guided Tour

◆

DOVER CASTLE KENT
A great royal fortress, one which symbolically dominates the towering white cliffs and the narrowest part of the English Channel, Dover Castle stands on terrain whose strategic value has been appreciated for 2000 years. Its outer walls follow the lines of an Iron Age hillfort, its precincts contain a Roman lighthouse and a Saxon church, and the medieval castle itself was altered and refortified right down to the 19th century, with drastic effects on its character and appearance.

Although King William is known to have fortified Dover shortly after the Battle of Hastings, the castle we can

View along the west walls to the tower keep at Dover

see now is essentially the superb structure built by Henry II in the 1180s and completed, with modifications, in the following century. At its heart stands Henry's great rectangular tower keep; 98 × 96 ft (30 × 29 m) in plan and 95 ft (28·9 m) high, it is a near-perfect cube, with boldly reinforced corners and pilaster strips centred on each wall. A tall, elaborate forebuilding controlled the entrance to the keep's three storeys; the top two were, as usual, residential suites consisting of two rooms divided by an internal cross-wall that also served to strengthen the structure. The upper residential storey was evidently designed for use by the King himself, although its loftiness is now concealed by 19th-century brickwork inserted to make the roof safe to use as an artillery platform.

There is evidence everywhere that the keep was intended to be exceptionally comfortable as well as exceptionally grand. The immense thickness of the walls (17–21 ft; 5–6·4 m) made it possible to provide many additional private rooms, passages and stairs, cut into the wall; each suite included a chapel with much striking carved decoration; there were fireplaces (although the present ones are 15th-century) and excellent privies; and lead pipes distributed water throughout the keep from a well-head on the top storey.

The keep stands within an oval bailey which is surrounded by a curtain wall. For this, Henry – or his master builder, Maurice the Engineer – employed the new idea of strongpointing the wall by equipping it at intervals with projecting towers from which flanking fire could reach any part of the 'field' outside. The inner curtain has ten such towers, in addition to two sets of towers flanking the gateways to north and south, which were also protected by barbicans. (Only the north barbican survives.) Dover Castle is therefore a curious hybrid, combining the passive last-resort defensive capability of the keep with the active principle associated with keepless strong-curtain castles (castles of enceinte).

Henry also began the outer curtain on the north-east side of the castle. The surviving portion, with two rectangular towers, runs parallel with the inner curtain – which suggests that the King may already have grasped the principle of the concentric castle, only applied elsewhere in Britain in any significant way from the 1270s. Henry's youngest son, King John, completed the outer curtain.

Dover Castle underwent its only testing siege in 1216, at the end of John's troubled reign. The forces of Prince Louis of France succeeded in bringing down one tower of the principal gateway, built by John at the northern apex of the outer curtain; and although the garrison managed to block the gap and hold out, John's successor, Henry III, took energetic measures to eliminate this weak point. His were the last really major medieval works at Dover. A complex, mighty gatehouse, the Constable's Tower, was built on the safer western side of the curtain as the new main entrance. The triple Norfolk Towers blocked King John's gateway, St John's Tower was built in the ditch in front of it, and fortifications were erected on the high land commanding it. Finally, these defences were interconnected by underground works, now eminently visitable as an audio-guided tour.

In the centre of Dover, on the A2
(map page 61)

ROMAN LIGHTHOUSE

CONSTABLE'S GATE

NEWEL STAIRS IN KEEP

Continued from page 93

tower with a large, but low, civilian Jacobean dwelling. Standing above the River Dee about 10 miles (16 km) from Aberdeen, the Tower of Drum was built to protect the Forest of Drum, one of the Scottish kings' favourite hunting-grounds during the Middle Ages. It is 70 ft (21 m) high (although its great bulk gives it a relatively squat appearance), rectangular, with rounded corners and curiously high merlons on the battlements; the walls are 12 ft (3·5 m) thick at the base, slimming down to 9 ft (2·75 m) – and thereby creating more space inside – on the upper storeys. As usual, entry to the tower was originally at first-floor level by a removable outside staircase. There is evidence to suggest that the construction of the tower was directed by Richard the Mason (Richard Cementarius; *fl.* 1264), the first recorded Provost of Aberdeen. In a surviving charter dated 1 February 1323, Robert the Bruce gave the tower and estate to his armour-bearer and clerk, William de Irwin, as a reward for his loyal service during the war of independence. Thereafter the Irwins mutated into Irvines, remaining in occupation at Drum for six and a half centuries. In 1619 the Jacobean house was added, its long roofs reflecting the greater availability of timber for building, thanks to the development of trade between north-east Scotland and the Baltic. Although much altered in the 17th and 18th centuries, the castle was carefully restored in the 1870s. In 1976 the widow of the last Irvine laird gave it to the National Trust for Scotland.

11 miles (17.5 km) west of Aberdeen, on the A93 (map page 63)

◆

Dunnottar Castle   grampian

Over the centuries this superb natural defensive site was built upon and fiercely contested until the Pax Britannica rendered its strengths obsolete. The ruins of the castle stand on a great flat-topped rock surrounded on three sides by the sea, with only a single, highly exposed path dipping and then rising up to the entrance. One of Scotland's great heroes, William Wallace, captured Dunnottar in 1297, but

Dunnottar – abandoned after the doomed 1715 rebellion

the earliest surviving building on the site is the keep erected by Sir William Keith, Earl Marischal of Scotland, at the end of the 14th century. Roofless but still standing almost to its original height, it was a tower house of the relatively new 'L'-type plan – effectively a rectangular tower with a wing added to provide extra accommodation. Despite its commanding position, a later Earl Marischal strengthened the entrance in 1575 with a very powerful gatehouse, and this was followed by yet more activity, notably an impressive quadrangle of buildings raised on the seaward side of the rock. Dunnottar was now not only a fortress but a palace. Caught up in the shifting allegiances characteristic of the 17th-century troubles, the castle kept the Royalist Earl of Montrose at bay in 1645, then endured the most famous siege in its history on behalf of Charles II in 1651–2; the 69-man garrison surrendered to the English Parliamentary forces, but only after holding out for eight months and smuggling the royal regalia to safety. In 1685 a less savoury episode – a kind of 'Black Hole of Dunnottar' – involved the imprisonment for two months in a single dungeon of 167 Covenanting men and women; a number of them perished from a combination of stifling heat, ill-treatment and lack of food, while others suffered cruel tortures to punish them for attempting to escape. In 1715 the current

Earl Marischal joined the doomed Jacobite rebellion and, as a result, when it was all over Dunnottar was slighted and abandoned.

17 miles (27 km) south of Aberdeen, on
the A92 (map page 63)

◆

DUNSTANBURGH CASTLE   NORTHUMBERLAND

Broken, bleak and isolated, Dunstanburgh epitomizes the romantic ruin, still physically as well as spiritually remote from the modern world: as in times past, it is still only to be reached by a route along the seashore, on foot or astride a beast of burden. Most of the remains date from 1313–22, when Thomas, Earl of Lancaster, built a mighty fortress on what appears to have been virgin ground until that time. Since cliffs and sea protected the site on its north side, Thomas's workmen cut a ditch 80 ft (24 m) wide, running very roughly south-west to north, that effectively converted the site into an island. Even more remarkably, his masons built a curtain wall with towers and turrets behind the ditch; and despite war and weather, some impressive stretches survive, along with the well-preserved Lilburn Tower, protecting the castle's long east flank, and two other towers. The Earl's mighty gatehouse survives as a huge fragment   two massive stumps with jagged fingers pointing at the sky. Unluckily for Thomas, the turbulent leader of the barons opposed to Edward II, he was unwilling or unable to take refuge at Dunstanburgh when fortune turned against him, and in 1322 he was captured, tried and executed.

The only other changes at Dunstanburgh were made in the 1380s by another member of the house of Lancaster, John of Gaunt. He had the entrance to the gatehouse blocked in so that it became a keep, put up a new gateway on one side of it protected by a barbican, and turned the area immediately behind the old and new gates into a small irregular quadrangle or inner bailey by adding two curtain walls and a square tower at the corner where they met. Dunstanburgh was a major Lancastrian fortress during the Wars of the Roses, frequently changing hands and receiving a battering by artillery from which it never really recovered.

On the coast, 8 miles (13 km) north-
east of Alnwick, via the B1340
(map page 62)

◆

DUNSTER CASTLE   SOMERSET

With a picturesquely varied skyline of battlements and towers, thick woodland all about it and the village of Dunster lying at its foot, this castle is a lovely sight. But its medieval air is deceptive, since it has passed through many phases of building and owes much of its present appearance to 19th-century nostalgia for the age of chivalry. There was indeed a castle here within a few years of the Norman Conquest, put up by William de Mohun, and in the 12th century it was rebuilt in stone. The Mohuns remained in possession until their line became extinct in 1404, and from then until 1976, when Dunster passed to the National Trust, it belonged to the Luttrell family; this occupation by only two families in over 900 years must be something of a record. Like so many others, Dunster Castle deteriorated in the 15th and 16th centuries, but it was brought up to contemporary standards of comfort and convenience in the early 1700s, when George Luttrell inserted

Dunster Castle, many times rebuilt over the centuries

a Jacobean mansion into the old structure.

During the Civil War the castle remained formidable enough to stand out for a time against a Parliamentary force led by Robert Blake (later more famous as a Cromwellian admiral), in spite of which its slighting in 1651 seems to have been relatively mild, mainly affecting the curtain wall. In 1683 Colonel Francis Luttrell gave Dunster two of its greatest treasures – a superbly carved oak staircase and a plasterwork dining-room ceiling, both with elaborate, consummately executed scenes featuring animals and foliage. Later occupants continued to add to the fabric, leaving a 13th-century gateway and a 15th-century gatehouse as the principal medieval remains. However, in 1868 the architect Anthony Salvin was called in to transform Dunster into an up-to-date country residence, which he did in typical Victorian fashion by combining the latest creature comforts with the immaculate 'medieval' exteriors that give the castle its present charm.

3 miles (5 km) south-east of Minehead,
on the A396 (map page 60)

◆

DUNVEGAN CASTLE   HIGHLAND

Dunvegan stands in a beautiful setting, on a rock above a harbour on the west coast of the Isle of Skye, and although the Victorian exterior of the castle is a little disappointing, this is only the outermost layer of a building that grew up over 600 years. In the late 13th century Leod, son of the King of Man, came here and put up a strong wall round the rock; he was the first chief of the MacLeods, and ever since then Dunvegan has been the seat of the head of the clan. The third chief erected a square keep in the 14th century, and in the 16th century Alasdair Crotach built the Fairy Tower – both incorporated in the present castle.

Dunvegan saw little action except for an occasional bloody clash with the MacDonalds (the MacLeods' traditional foes), but it retained its fortress character down to 1748, being accessible only from the loch via a well-defended sea-gate. A landward front entrance was created in time for a well-known visit by Dr Johnson and his future biographer, James Boswell, during which the laird's wife complained that Dunvegan was 'a rude place', and that it was 'a Herculean labour to make a dinner here'. The 23rd laird, back from India with a young bride, did much to remedy this state of affairs, and also began the planting that led to the present woods and gardens; and during the Victorian period the castle was completely modernized. But it is still the home of the clan chiefs, and filled with relics of a colourful past, from the mysterious, centuries-old Fairy Flag to the stays of the Jacobite heroine Flora MacDonald.

On the Isle of Skye, 1½ miles (2.5 km)
north-west of Dunvegan, on the A850
(map page 63)

◆

DURHAM CASTLE   COUNTY DURHAM

The fame and splendour of Durham's cathedral make it easy to overlook – or at any rate ignore – the castle just across the Palace Green. Yet both buildings contribute to the city's spectacular skyline, rising up from a high sandstone bluff above a loop in the River Wear; and both need to be seen if the visitor is to appreciate the distinctive role played by medieval Durham. Like the cathedral, the castle was the property of the Bishops of Durham, and it served as a mighty fortress-palace for a line of ecclesiastics who were also formidable territorial magnates; they ruled a large expanse of the North, the Palatinate of Durham, enjoying a near-complete autonomy, with their own courts and coinage, in return for their readiness to raise an army against the Scots.

The great castle erected by the 12th-century bishops replaced the first stone buildings, ordered by William the Conqueror in the 1070s; of these, the lovely chapel survives, and constitutes one of the high points of any visit. The basic layout of Durham Castle was and is an octagonal keep on a mound and a bailey enclosed by curtain walls. But there

Right Dunvegan – seat of the MacLeod clan for over 600 years

were many additions in the 13th century, including a great hall – one of the largest in Britain – that dwarfed the existing Norman halls. The 14th century brought a new keep, built by Bishop Hatfield, and alterations, embellishments and new buildings continued to be executed over the generations, culminating in the virtual rebuilding of the keep in the early 19th century. This makes a guided tour of the buildings very welcome; and it is also inescapable, for the castle has been part of Durham University since 1832, when the Palatinate was abolished.

In the centre of the city, off the A177
(map page 62)

EASTNOR CASTLE   HEREFORD AND WORCESTER

Eastnor is an early example of 19th-century Gothic fantasy on the grand scale, contemporary with the historical novels of Sir Walter Scott which gave such an impetus to the cult of the Middle Ages. In 1812 the 2nd Lord Somers commissioned a leading architect, Sir Robert Smirke, to build him a 'medieval' castle. No expense was spared. A man-made lake was created to provide a suitable setting, and mules carried the necessary stone all the way from the Forest of Dean. Although Smirke's intention was to make a faithful copy of a medieval castle, the final result was a severe, grey edifice that still has a surprisingly clean-cut appearance, emphasized by the slender towers and broad battlements with exaggerated merlons.

The interior was equally dominated by fantasy, since the presence of contemporary rooms for living in (drawing room and dining room) did not inhibit Somers and Smirke from constructing an enormous great hall for non-existent feudal retainers. Some 60 ft (18 m) long and 55 ft (16·5 m) high, with a pleasantly arcaded gallery on the first floor, it now contains the large collection of arms and armour accumulated by the 3rd Lord Somers. The drawing room was redecorated by one of the great Victorian apostles of the Gothic

Eastnor Castle, designed by Sir Robert Smirke

style, A.W.N. Pugin, shortly before his death in 1852; it is a lavish, virtuoso farewell performance, with the slender fan vaulting characteristic of the later Middle Ages, great brass chandeliers, and a riotous profusion of gilding and heraldic emblems. By contrast, the library is richly decorated but in a cheerfully secular Renaissance style. Altogether Eastnor is a fascinating place, testifying to the immense wealth and self-confidence of a governing class unafraid to turn its fantasies into huge, durable realities.

10 miles (16 km) south-west of Great
Malvern, via the A449 and A438
(map pages 60–1)

———————◆———————

EDINBURGH CASTLE LOTHIAN

This famous, much-visited castle stands on a hill (the core of an extinct volcano) that falls away steeply on three sides and slopes down on the fourth (east) side to meet Edinburgh's Old Town. Although occupied since at least the 6th century, the site has been so fought-over, built and rebuilt upon that little survives from its early history. A castle here was occupied by the English for 12 years after the capture of the Scots king William the Lion outside ALNWICK CASTLE (Northumberland) in 1174, and it fell again in 1296 to Edward I, 'the Hammer of the Scots'. In 1313 it was demolished as part of Robert the Bruce's policy of destroying any stronghold that might be useful to the invader, but an exception was made for the 12th-century chapel dedicated to the canonized Scottish queen, St Margaret, which is consequently the earliest surviving structure in Edinburgh Castle.

It was the 16th- and early 17th-century buildings and defences, erected on the castle's vulnerable east side, that became its core. They confront the visitor after he or she has crossed the Esplanade (an 18th-century parade ground on which the annual Tattoo is now held) and passed through the 19th-century outer gateway. Looming above the route into the castle are the mighty Half-Moon and Forewall Batteries (1570s), massive walls supporting an artillery

Edinburgh Castle, scene of many a battle over the centuries

platform from which raking fire could be directed at an attacker who assaulted the Portcullis Gate (19th-century, but replacing a 16th-century original). Then, just inside the gate, the steep Lang Stairs lead up to the courtyard (Crown Square) in which James IV's great hall and palace face the later Queen Anne Barracks and Scottish National War Memorial. The great hall was restored with overly-romantic enthusiasm in the 19th century, but its original splendid timber roof is still intact. Even more impressive are the extensive underground vaults that were raised to create the level surface on which the hall and palace stand; these have been used over the centuries as storerooms and prisons, and one of them now holds Mons Meg, a giant 15th-century siege-gun brought into action on several notable occasions.

In the centre of the city, off the A1
(map page 63)

———————◆———————

EDZELL CASTLE TAYSIDE

The dour remains of this castle stand as a monument to the Lindsay Earls of Crawford. They became lords of Edzell in 1357, but the earliest part of the present structure is the keep or tower house, erected at the beginning of the 16th century. It still rises through four storeys to the level of the highly decorative corbels that once supported the parapet, and contains a fine hall that was lavishly furnished until the 18th century, when the Lindsays' creditors stripped it of everything saleable.

Towards the end of the 16th century the 9th Earl of Crawford built out to the north and east of the keep, adding a range of buildings (now very ruinous) and a wall; consequently, Edzell was transformed into a courtyard castle, more up to date and more comfortable than before, but still geared to self-defence.

In 1604 the trend towards luxury and sophistication was carried much further by Sir David Lindsay, the 9th Earl's son, who added the large walled garden or 'pleasance' which is now the castle's main attraction for most visitors, since the ornamental walls are in good condition and the formal garden is laid out in strict 17th-century style. Its most original features are the decorations on the walls – heraldic patterns of masonry with the Lindsay chequers and stars, niches for statuary, and a series of stone panels carved in low relief and representing the Cardinal Virtues, Liberal Arts and Celestial Deities; these were apparently seen by Lindsay at Nuremberg and copied for him. However, the garden's summer house shows that its builder's attitudes remained ambiguous, for this pleasure-place is turreted and equipped with gun-loops.

8 miles (13 km) north of Brechin, off
the B966 (map page 63)

EILEAN DONAN CASTLE HIGHLAND

There is no more romantically situated castle in Britain than Eilean Donan, which stands on a tiny island at the entrance to lovely Loch Duich, facing the Isle of Skye. But although the site has a long history, the castle that we now see is mainly a creation of 20th-century nostalgia. The earliest known fortress here was a 13th-century castle of enceinte, built to deter Norse raiders who still harried the coasts; and in the next century its defences were strengthened by the addition of a rectangular keep in the north-east corner of the wall. Later Eilean Donan became the stronghold of the MacKenzie Earls of Seaforth, surviving well enough until disaster struck in 1719: the Jacobite 5th Earl came out for the Old Pretender and installed a Spanish garrison in the castle, which was bombarded and destroyed by three English frigates.

Subsequently, the ruins of Eilean Donan were much admired, and there were those who regretted the extensive – and immensely expensive – rebuilding undertaken by Colonel John MacRae, appropriately enough a descendant of the MacRaes whom the Earls of Seaforth had habitually put in charge of the old castle. The work was carried out over two decades from 1912, and the keep and other parts of Eilean Donan were restored in a rugged style that time has already made to seem convincingly medieval. A modern bridge and causeway link the island with the mainland. As well as displaying various Highland impedimenta, the castle serves as a Clan MacRae war memorial.

10 miles (16 km) east of Kyle of
Lochalsh, on the A87 (map page 63)

FARNHAM CASTLE SURREY

Farnham Castle was part of a valuable estate that belonged for centuries to the bishopric of Winchester, and there was a bishop in residence here until 1955. The fabric has consequently been well looked after, and buildings have multiplied inside the triangular area which was formerly the bailey. For castle enthusiasts, however, the most fascinating part is the great round keep and motte. The 30 ft (9 m) high motte was put up in about 1138 for Bishop Henry of Blois, the brother of King Stephen. Excavations have shown that his tower (now vanished) was not placed on the motte, but was built up from ground level within it, so that the mound helped to shore up the tower rather than riskily bearing its weight.

A stone square now marks the place where the tower

Continued on page 106

Guided Tour

GLAMIS CASTLE   TAYSIDE

In many respects Scotland's finest historic house, Glamis Castle is also famous as the fictional setting of Shakespeare's *Macbeth* and the actual childhood home of Queen Elizabeth, the Queen Mother. It has been occupied by the same family for over 600 years, ever since Sir John Lyon became thane of Glamis in 1372. Sir John, who married the daughter of King Robert II, was subsequently murdered by his brother-in-law; but the family survived the turbulent Scottish Middle Ages, becoming lords of Glamis (1445) and Earls of Kinghorne (1606) and Strathmore (1677). After the marriage of the 9th Earl to the Bowes heiress (1767) the family assumed the name Bowes Lyon, by which it has been known ever since.

Surprisingly, Glamis stands in very unfortress-like fashion on flat ground at the bottom of the Vale of Strathmore; a possible explanation lies in its origin as a royal hunting lodge, sited mainly with the pleasures of the chase in mind. However, although Glamis has been extended and rebuilt over the centuries, a 14th-century private fortress does survive at its heart. This is a strong, compact, rectangular block with a short wing built at right angles on to its south face, forming the characteristic 'L'-plan Scottish tower house. It is still the visual focus of the approach to the castle, since the main entrance is in the re-entrant (inner) angle of the 'L', which is occupied by a 17th-century round stair tower.

The 17th-century extensions to the old tower house consisted essentially of two further 'L'-plan blocks, to the west and to the east, each finished off with a round tower in the far corner. The west wing, burned down in 1800, was rebuilt shortly afterwards, possibly by the well-known architect James Wyatt. Visitors enter this wing first, from the north, and are shown the huge first-floor dining room.

By contrast with its 19th-century opulence, the Crypt retains something of the rugged atmosphere of the tower house, of which it was the hall. Originally the only access to it was by a narrow stairway, wide enough to admit – and to be efficiently defended by – a single man; at its bottom was the indispensable well. Below the Crypt are the main entrance, guarded by a yett (an iron-grid door), and the old kitchen with its huge fireplace.

Also old and austere is Duncan's Hall, named with imaginative licence after Macbeth's royal victim; it is thought to have served as a room for retainers set to guard the former hall. Portraits of James V of Scotland and his queen on one wall

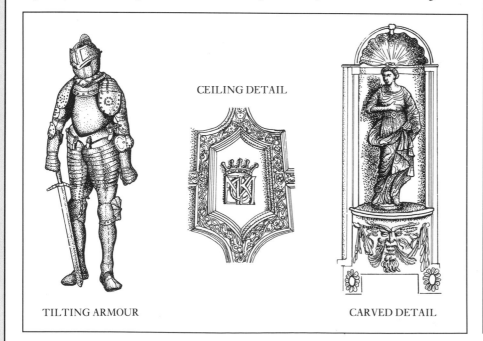

TILTING ARMOUR

CEILING DETAIL

CARVED DETAIL

recall the nadir of the Lyon fortunes, when the King occupied and stripped Glamis after he had unjustly condemned the widowed Lady Glamis to be burned as a witch in 1540. Her young son survived – just – because he managed to outlive the King.

Despite some intense and expensive involvement in the troubles of the period, the lords of Glamis prospered greatly during the 17th century. This is reflected in the drawing room – a splendid showpiece, formerly more aptly known as the great hall, with a magnificent plasterwork ceiling, huge fireplace and very fine portraits. It is presided over by the 3rd Earl in curious fleshy armour, painted with his sons and his hounds and pointing to Glamis as it was in his day, with impressive long-vanished outer walls and gates.

Among the many other rooms crammed with noteworthy sights or exhibits are the chapel with panels painted by de Wet, the billiard room, 'King Malcolm's Room', and the Blue Room, which contains Jacobite relics such as the sword presented to the family by the Old Pretender when he stayed at the house, and the watch he

The splendid entrance front of Glamis Castle

---

inadvertently left there under his pillow. All kinds of interests are catered for by the royal apartments, prepared for the then Duke and Duchess of York, later King George VI and Queen Elizabeth, *née* Bowes Lyon.

12 miles (19 km) north of Dundee, via the A929 and A928 (map page 63)

Continued from page 103

stood; like other castles erected by overmighty subjects during Stephen's reign, it was demolished by his successor, Henry II, in about 1155. Later in the century it was replaced by a six-towered shell keep of unusual type, built around the base of the mound instead of its top; the mound was subsequently levelled off to eliminate the gap between earth and wall.

In 1216–17, during the confused period following the death of King John, Farnham was captured for a time by the French. The 17th-century Civil War was more destructive: after changing hands several times the castle was slighted, as the gap in its east side testifies. Many changes were made over the centuries in the domestic accommodation at Farnham, much of which has an engaging late 17th-century character; however, the most striking building, standing guard over the rest, is the tall brick tower put up by Bishop Waynflete in 1470–75.

Half a mile (1 km) north of the town
centre, off the A287 (map page 61)

———————◆———————

FRAMLINGHAM CASTLE   SUFFOLK

Despite later alterations and additions, Framlingham remains essentially the great baronial stronghold built in the late 12th century for the Bigods, East Anglian magnates who for two centuries played a leading role in English politics, often in turbulent opposition to the Crown. Henry II demolished a timber fortress put up by the Bigods at Framlingham, where they had been in possession since the beginning of the 12th century; but soon after this strong king's death in 1189, Roger Bigod, 2nd Earl of Norfolk, asserted his independence by rebuilding at Framlingham in stone, on a new principle, and on the grand scale.

The central feature of the new castle was its huge and splendid oval of curtain wall, which was powerfully reinforced by no less than 13 open-backed rectangular towers. This was a very early English example of a castle design based on active defence of strong, high curtain walls rather than a passive holding-out inside a keep. At Framlingham

Framlingham Castle, built in the late 12th century

the builders took the concept to its logical conclusion by dispensing entirely with the keep, while remaining old-fashioned enough to put up rectangular towers, which were already known to be more vulnerable than round ones.

Framlingham shared the unstable fortunes of the Bigods, and in 1216 it was besieged and captured by King John. Later in the century the Bigods disappeared from history, and the castle eventually passed to the Howards. Well endowed as Dukes of Norfolk and Earls of Arundel, they made little use of Framlingham, but like other Howard holdings it was on several occasions in Tudor and Stuart times forfeited to the Crown and later recovered.

The bridge into the castle, and the red-brick, barley-sugar-twist chimneys that rise so oddly from the walls and towers, are relics of this period. In 1636 Framlingham was bequeathed to Pembroke College, Cambridge, and in accordance with the conditions laid down, a poorhouse was built that still forms part of the later hall sheltering behind the west curtain; it now houses a local museum. Pembroke College presented Framlingham to the nation in 1912.

On the north side of the town, 19 miles
(30.5 km) north-east of Ipswich, via the
A12 and B1116 (map page 61)

———————◆———————

HARLECH CASTLE GWYNEDD

A favourite subject for painters, Harlech stands on a rock set above Tremadoc Bay and, viewed from the west, is a spectacular sight with the mountains of Snowdonia rising behind it. The castle was built very quickly (1283–9) for Edward I by his master mason, James of St George, who himself served as its constable in 1290–3. This was an appropriate reward, since Harlech was one of Master James's handsomest creations, a classic concentric fortress making surprisingly few concessions to the irregular terrain.

Its nucleus is a quadrangular inner ward surrounded by a high curtain wall with strong round towers at the corners and a powerful gatehouse in the middle of the east side. This was the sector most vulnerable to an attack from inland, and the gatehouse is mighty indeed, occupying most of the east side and dwarfing the actual castle entrance within it. The lower curtain wall around the outer ward is less well preserved, but it has an interesting large semicircular latrine on the south side. This projects out over the deep ditch cut into the rock to afford further protection on the landward east and south sides.

After Madog's rebellion (1294–5), during which Harlech was besieged, a third wall was put up around the base of the castle rock; steps hacked out of the dauntingly steep rock face linked the castle with the water gate in the outermost wall, giving access to the harbour (now vanished) and the aid from the sea that, in an emergency, might make the difference between survival and surrender.

Harlech has had a stirring, turbulent history. During Owain Glyndŵr's rebellion, his French allies gained control of the sea, and in 1404 the castle was forced to surrender to him (he held it until 1409). Later it was besieged for seven years (1461–8) before surrendering to the Yorkists during the Wars of the Roses – a feat of endurance commemorated in the song 'Men of Harlech'; and even in the Civil War it was held to the last for the King against Parliament.

In the town, 11 miles (17.5 km) north of
Barmouth, on the A496 (map page 60)

HEDINGHAM CASTLE ESSEX

The keep at Hedingham, guarding the crossing of the River Colne, serves as a memorial to the de Veres, one of the great baronial families of the Middle Ages. Aubrey de Vere took part in the Norman Conquest, and de Vere Earls of Oxford figured for centuries in English history, surviving all its ups and downs until their line died out naturally in 1703.

Hedingham, probably built in the 1130s, was the de Veres' principal stronghold, seemingly modelled on the archiepiscopal splendours of ROCHESTER CASTLE (Kent) and designed to show off both the owners' military strength and their command of comforts and luxuries. It still fulfils this function, in spite of the disappearance of the castle's baileys and the buildings inside them. For the sole survivor – the keep – is splendid: an imposing rectangular structure standing almost 100 ft (30 m) high, with two of the original corner towers and well-preserved decorative details on the outside. Few traces remain of the forebuilding which, as usual, gave access to the keep at first-floor level, but the interior is very impressive. A spiral staircase leads up to Hedingham's finest feature, the great hall. This is exceptionally spacious and lofty, since it occupies the entire floor (by contrast with ROCHESTER, divided by a cross-wall) and rises up through two storeys. Looking down on the hall is a gallery, cut into the 12 ft (3.5 m) thickness of the wall and running all the way round it. A great central arch, 28 ft (8.5 m) wide, supports the timber ceiling, adding to the impression of monumentality. All these things, in combination with the carved decoration and sparse furnishings, create an effect of rude but powerful baronial splendour.

4 miles (6.5 km) north of Halstead, via
the A604 and B1058 (map page 61)

HELMSLEY CASTLE NORTH YORKSHIRE

Despite its sad state of decay, Helmsley is an interesting castle whose basic layout is still easily identified; and its remains – especially the ruined keep – are peculiarly

Domestic range at Helmsley Castle in North Yorkshire

effective in evoking the pathos of vanished grandeur.

The outcrop of rock on which Helmsley stands may have determined its roughly rectangular plan, which was certainly in evidence after Robert de Roos put up a curtain wall and keep in about 1200. The curtain wall was equipped with strongly projecting round towers, to which a large square mural tower was added later in the 13th century. Two barbicans were built during the 13th century, and huge double-ditched and ramparted earthworks, still such a feature of Helmsley, were thrown up. The attractions of civilian life manifested themselves in the building of a 14th-century great hall and, during the Tudor period, a range of domestic buildings that ran away from the square tower, along the curtain wall towards the north-west.

Now the most striking single feature at Helmsley is certainly the keep. Almost all of it except for one straight side was destroyed when the castle was slighted after a three-month siege by the Parliamentarians during the Civil War; but that one side rises to its full height and defiantly continues to carry its two square turrets. The keep straddled the curtain wall and before its slighting was 'D'-shaped, a plan so unusual that it is somewhat mysterious; one plausible explanation is that it represents a timid step away from the isolated tower keep, towards the wall tower and great gatehouse that were to become the norm later in the 13th century.

24 miles (38 km) north of York, via
the B1363 and A170 (map page 62)

HERMITAGE CASTLE BORDERS

Lowering over the Hermitage Water, this is the archetypal border castle – a solid, unrelieved block of brown sandstone, with only a few unfriendly apertures looking out on to wild Liddesdale. During the Middle Ages it was a place of dark private deeds and public dispute, several times changing hands between Scots and English.

The first Hermitage Castle we know much about was an oblong early 14th-century structure erected around a small

Hermitage Castle, fiercely fought over in the Middle Ages

courtyard. A few decades later the Douglas lairds rebuilt it as a very large tower house occupying the same area; the truncated former courtyard façades became internal walls, and are still identifiable. The four-storey tower house was built on the 'L'-plan, as a rectangle with a single wing projecting at right angles; the addition of three square corner towers in about 1400 effectively completed the castle as it now stands. Images of long-forgotten affrays are evoked by an inconspicuous feature: the row of socket-holes at third-floor level on the outside, which once held the supports of a timber gallery from which the garrison could fire at or fling down lethal objects upon their attackers.

In 1492 the Douglases exchanged Hermitage for Bothwell Castle on the Clyde, and in time the most famous of the Earls of Bothwell came into possession, acting as lieutenant on the Borders for Mary, Queen of Scots. Since he was later to become her second husband, some historians have put a romantic interpretation on the famous occasion in October 1566 when Mary rode 50 miles from Jedburgh and back in a day to visit the wounded Bothwell; others, less romantic or more concerned for the Queen's reputation, see the visit as a necessary act of courtesy, and emphasize the fact that Mary hurried away, preferring not to stay overnight within the grim walls of Hermitage Castle!

18 miles (29 km) south of Hawick, on
the B6399 (map page 62)

Hever Castle and its moat from the north-west

HEVER CASTLE KENT

Neatly laid out on a rectangular platform within the waters of its moat, Hever is a very lovely fortified manor house. Its timeless picture-book Englishness was actually the creation – or re-creation – of a 20th-century American millionaire, William Waldorf Astor, who bought the estate in 1903. Astor employed the architect F. L. Pearson to undertake a major restoration of the house which was carried out in exemplary fashion.

Hever was built in the 14th century, and a royal permission to crenellate was forthcoming about 1340 (which does not exclude the possibility that some defences existed earlier); however, most of the serious fortifications, including the fine battlemented gatehouse and the moat, seem to have been constructed at the end of the century, when a second licence was issued. From 1462 the house was well maintained and even improved by the Bullens or Boleyns, a London business family that was fast coming up in the world. It was at Hever that Henry VIII adulterously pursued young Anne Boleyn, whom he first made his queen and later executed.

After the fall of the Boleyns the house passed to the Crown; it soon went into a decline, and by the 19th century had become a simple working farmhouse. Astor restored it, very effectively on the outside and perhaps a little too effectively within: the lavish woodwork, panelling and plasterwork, and the collections of paintings, sculptures, tapestries and armour, could only have been assembled by a modern millionaire. But all of these, like Hever's lovely gardens and lake, have a different kind of historical interest, as examples of the opulent nature of Edwardian fantasy.

10 miles (16 km) west of Tonbridge, via
the B2027 (map page 61)

◆

INVERARAY CASTLE STRATHCLYDE

Inveraray Castle represents a significant moment in the history of the Scottish castle – the moment when its fighting qualities, which had only recently become redundant, took on a romantic aura and inspired a new, nostalgic, mock-military type of building: the sham castle. There was a certain appropriateness in the fact that this occurred at Inveraray, for centuries the seat of the Campbell chiefs, who had successfully steered their way through wars and civil wars to become Dukes of Argyll and pillars of the 18th-century establishment.

The new castle was erected by the 3rd Duke from 1743, after designs by the architect Roger Morris, and at the same time the town of Inveraray was totally rebuilt on the Duke's orders. One became an example of rational Georgian urban planning; the other an exercise in Georgian fantasy. The castle is 'Gothick', a mock-medieval structure with more than a suggestion – strengthened by the later Victorian addition of attic dormer windows – of a Loire château; its blue-green granite and cone-topped towers would inspire many later essays in Scottish 'baronial' building.

After the rather stolid proportions of the exterior, the airy lightness of the classical interiors comes as a delightful surprise. They date from 1772–82, when the 5th Duke commissioned Robert Mylne to redecorate virtually the entire castle. Now, the beautifully painted panelled walls and elegant plasterwork ceilings of Inveraray provide a sumptuous setting for the fine Beauvais tapestries, French furniture, family portraits, and weapons and armour that make this stately home so attractive to visitors.

58 miles (93 km) north-west of
Glasgow, via the A82 and A83
(map page 63)

◆

KENILWORTH CASTLE WARWICKSHIRE

Kenilworth is a ruin, but a great and glorious one that has witnessed some high moments in English history. The first stone castle here was built by Henry I's treasurer, Geoffrey de Clinton, in the early 12th century. The strong, square keep and walled bailey were sufficiently formidable to persuade Henry II to annex them, and in about 1205 King John created a second bailey by adding an outer

The 'Leicester Buildings' at Kenilworth Castle in Warwickshire

curtain wall. At some time over the next few years Kenilworth was provided with a vast lake on three sides which made it one of the greatest fortresses in the kingdom.

Its capacity to resist was demonstrated in 1266, when the son of Simon de Montfort held out at Kenilworth for six months against forces led by the Lord Edward, Henry III's son (and later King Edward I); starvation eventually compelled the surrender of the castle, but only after the besiegers had offered generous terms. In the 1370s John of Gaunt, Duke of Lancaster and brother to Edward III, spent huge sums of money to make Kenilworth into a show-castle worthy of a royal prince, adding a great hall, a chapel, towers and other finely executed buildings along the line of the inner curtain, to the south of the keep. Finally, Robert Dudley, Earl of Leicester – Elizabeth I's 'Sweet Robin' – transformed the castle into a palace capable of housing the entire court.

The 'Leicester Buildings', next to Gaunt's range, were put up by the Earl, as were the stable block with its decorative timberwork and the great gatehouse just beyond the keep in the outer curtain. In 1575 Kenilworth became the setting for one of the most lavish entertainments ever given in England – a 19-day jamboree of music, dancing, plays, pageants, allegories, masques, dumb-shows, bear-baiting, fireworks and addresses, staged by Leicester for the Queen. Like so many other castles, Kenilworth was slighted by Parliament in 1649 and abandoned; the thoroughgoing destruction of the north outer curtain and north wall of the keep is still obvious to the eye. But all these buildings survive in ruined grandeur, and still inspire admiration.

On the west side of the town, 5 miles (8 km) south-west of Coventry, on the A429 (map page 61)

KIDWELLY CASTLE DYFED

A mighty ruin which gives an impression of immense contained strength, Kidwelly Castle stands within its tight girdle of walls on a ridge above the River Gwendraeth.

The mighty ruins of Kidwelly Castle

Only its banks and ditches now recall the Norman castle built here by Bishop Roger of Salisbury in the early 12th century. The castle later changed hands – and form – many times, and the earliest surviving structure dates from the mid 1270s, when the returned crusader Pain de Chaworth built an up-to-date courtyard castle with a quadrangular curtain wall defended by a strong projecting round tower at each corner. After 1298, when he married the Chaworth heiress, Henry of Lancaster added some domestic apartments and one of Kidwelly's most striking features the chapel tower, built out on to the slope down to the river and buttressed by two great sharp-edged 'spurs' of masonry.

Early in the 14th century Kidwelly was converted into a concentric castle when a semicircular outer curtain wall with four towers and two double-towered gatehouses was thrown round Pain's fortress. The principal, southern gatehouse was, and is, an asymmetrical giant – tremendously impressive but of dubious military value, since it was not completed for over a century. One interesting result of building the new, high curtain wall was that the inner towers had to be raised to enable the defenders to fire over it – an operation that has left the up-down-up-down contours of the earlier battlements still visible to the naked eye within the masonry.

Kidwelly Castle passed its only serious military test in 1403, when Owain Glyndŵr's forces attacked it in vain.

Despite some later rebuilding, it was virtually abandoned by the beginning of the 17th century.

In the town, 7 miles (11 km) west of
Llanelly, via the B4308 (map page 60)

KIRBY MUXLOE CASTLE LEICESTERSHIRE

There is no more poignant witness to the fickleness of fortune than Kirby Muxloe Castle. It was built for William, Lord Hastings, who had risen to be Lord Chamberlain of England under Edward IV. To celebrate his eminence, Hastings was already fortifying his manor at Ashby de la Zouch with a tower house when he decided to embark on this more ambitious exercise in self-glorification. In October 1480 workmen began clearing the site at Kirby Muxloe and digging a 70 ft (21 m) wide moat; and in the following summer the master mason John Couper arrived to begin building in earnest. Kirby Muxloe was intended to be a brick castle laid out on a regular courtyard plan, with rectangular curtain walls, corner towers, wall towers midway along three sides and a great gatehouse dominating the fourth. Matters went forward steadily enough until 13 June 1483, two months after the death of Edward IV, when the new Lord Protector, Richard of Gloucester (soon to make himself king as Richard III), summarily arrested and executed Hastings on the same day. After this, the only work done on the site was small-scale activity designed to protect the existing fabric; when it came to an end in December 1484, £1088 had been spent on the project.

Today, Kirby Muxloe is not very different from the way John Couper left it, with one completed square corner tower, a large, truncated, rectangular gatehouse with four octagonal turrets in its corners, and the foundations of walls and towers that were never built. As is so often the case, it is not easy to say how seriously the castle was intended to serve as a fortress. The stone dressings and the black patterns in the brickwork are not necessarily symptoms of frivolity, but no great reliance can have been placed on the resistant quality of the thin brickwork; and the gunports,

although numerous, are not very convincingly located: some in the tower point straight at the gatehouse and, if fired through, might have missed the enemy but would certainly have damaged the castle!

4 miles (6.5 km) west of Leicester, via
the A47 and B5380 (map page 61)

LAUNCESTON CASTLE CORNWALL

Now a small market town, Launceston was a considerable place in the Middle Ages, and one well worth guarding with a strong castle. Strategically sited on the eastern border of Cornwall, it became the administrative centre of this far-western Celtic realm – a remote, tin-rich area whose security was normally entrusted only to a member of the royal family.

The first post-Conquest fortification here was a timber castle built by King William's brother, Robert of Mortain, whose workforce threw up the huge, dauntingly steep motte on which the present ruins stand; it was in the north-east corner of the large, oblong bailey, now a town park known as the Castle Green. At Launceston the transition to stone was made surprisingly late – around 1200, when a shell keep was erected on the top of the motte.

This relatively unambitious scheme was drastically changed a few decades later, when the King's brother, Richard, Earl of Cornwall, swept away the internal buildings and put up a high round tower inside and rising clear of the shell wall. It is this keep-within-a-keep arrangement, an early form of concentric defence, that chiefly survives and gives Launceston its special quality. In Richard's time the space between the tower and the shell was roofed over, providing a second fighting platform in addition to the tower top; moreover, just beyond the shell keep he built a lower wall (now gone) to serve as a third defensive line. Access to the stone steps up the mound was controlled by a gatehouse which survives, although the various portcullises that

Right *The shell keep and round tower of Launceston Castle*

hampered the intruder have vanished.

All that remains of the bailey are a few sections of wall and a gatehouse in its south side. History passed Launceston by, and the castle was left to decay until the Civil War, when it was fiercely contested, changed hands several times, and was badly damaged. In the 1720s the novelist Daniel Defoe found it 'all in ruins and heaps of rubbish'. The 20th century has thankfully removed the rubbish and revealed the grandeur of the ruins.

**Close to the town centre, 42 miles
(67 km) west of Exeter, on the A30
(map page 60)**

◆

LEEDS CASTLE   KENT

Often called the loveliest of all castles, Leeds has a long romantic façade stretching out over two islands in a lake and pierced by the arches of the covered bridge that links them; its park and woodland setting completes the picture of a perfect antique beauty. But in reality Leeds Castle has been much altered over the centuries; and major 19th- and 20th-century rebuildings and restorations are responsible for a good deal of what appears to be medieval, even if the final effect is such as to disarm criticism. The main

Leeds Castle, built in the 1270s by Edward I

part of the castle stands on the nearer, much larger island which served as the bailey, its picturesquely varied buildings and walls surrounding a large green. Across the bridge, the sturdy keep, known as the gloriette, rises directly out of the water, its dour medieval walls now broken by the fine Tudor bay windows.

There was a Norman castle at Leeds in the 12th century, but the present structure originated with Edward I, who built the castle in the 1270s and probably devised the water defences by damming the little River Len. He presented Leeds to Queen Eleanor, and the castle became a customary part of the dower of English queens down to the beginning of the 15th century. Henry VIII converted it into a Tudor palace, among other things building the Maiden's Tower for the royal maids of honour.

Tapestries, Impressionist paintings and other items add to the charm of the interiors, although there is not much that has any significant connection with the castle's history; even the 16th-century staircase with a figure of a crusader is a modern importation. Outside, with its gardens, duckery, golf course and, most recently, maze and grotto, Leeds aims to attract and succeeds very well; but although the castle boasts a unique collection of medieval dog collars, the descendants of the wearers are not welcome as visiting members of the public.

**4 miles (6.5 km) east of Maidstone, via
the M20 and B2163 (map page 61)**

◆

LEWES CASTLE   EAST SUSSEX

Lewes is most unusual in possessing two castle-mounds, one at each end of an oval bailey running roughly south-west to north-east. Such an arrangement would divide (and therefore overtax) the resources of most Norman lords, and it is probably significant that only one of the mottes seems to have been built on when the transition to stone was made. This occurred very early – before 1100 – because Lewes guarded a gap in the South Downs through which an invader might march on London. For this reason, William

Lewes Castle, which once stood guard over the South Downs

the Conqueror entrusted the Rape of Lewes to one of his closest, most loyal followers, William de Warenne, who built a castle close to the River Ouse. (The Rape was an administrative district peculiar to Sussex.) His son, another William, put up a shell keep on the south-west motte; only part of it survives, but it is a splendid fragment, much dignified by two semi-octagonal towers added in the 13th century.

Not much of the curtain walls and towers remains, but there is a fine, sturdy, well-preserved barbican that was added in the early 14th century to take over the gatehouse function of the modest Norman tower. This proved to be a sad, final flourish. Soon afterwards, in 1347, the Warenne line died out, and the castle was abandoned and never reoccupied. Damaged in riots and plundered by local people for building materials, its fabric deteriorated for centuries until it came under the protection of the Sussex Archaeological Association.

In the town, 8 miles (13 km) north-east
of Brighton, via the A27 (map page 61)

◆

LINDISFARNE CASTLE   NORTHUMBERLAND

Lindisfarne Castle is a fine romantic sight, dominating the Holy Island from the heights of Beblowe Crag. However, it was a relative latecomer to the island, which had been celebrated throughout Europe between the 7th and 9th centuries as a seat of monastic learning and piety. Subsequently, a Benedictine priory stood on the island from 1082 until the Dissolution of the Monasteries by Henry VIII in 1536–9. Shortly afterwards Henry decided to build an artillery fort to guard the island's harbour – in those days of some commercial and strategic importance – from the Scots and French; and the economically-minded masons used the abandoned priory's stones as building materials and the priory church as a storehouse.

Lindisfarne Castle never saw much action, and the garrison had dwindled to seven men by 1715, when two enterprising Jacobites disrupted its sleepy routines by taking it over and holding out overnight in heroic, if slightly ridicu-

Lindisfarne Castle, dominating the island

lous fashion. In 1819, with the Napoleonic Wars at an end, the castle's guns were removed and it was allowed to decay. In 1901 it was bought by Edward Hudson, the successful proprietor of the magazine *Country Life*, and he engaged Edwin Lutyens, then a rising young architect, to restore Lindisfarne Castle while simultaneously turning it into a comfortable contemporary home.

Lutyens' technical skill and romantic sensibility were of a high order, and he created the present dwelling with its rock passages and vaulted rooms affording superb views from the Crag. Whether he was quite as successful in combining this with real domestic comfort is another matter. Although it is still furnished, and the wall garden designed by Gertrude Jekyll is carefully looked after, Lindisfarne Castle has not been lived in since 1968 and is maintained by the National Trust solely for the enjoyment of the public.

13 miles (21 km) south-east of Berwick-upon-
Tweed, off the A1 at Beal (map page 62)

◆

LOCH LEVEN CASTLE   TAYSIDE

A small, grim stronghold in a broad, bleak landscape, Loch Leven Castle has figured in many episodes of Scottish history. It stands on a little island at the west end of the loch (a National Nature Reserve since 1964) and is reached by ferry during the summer. Because of a fall in the water level, the island now extends beyond the castle walls, making it look less formidable and romantic than it did in its heyday.

There was a royal residence here even in the 13th century, for in 1257 a faction anxious to control the young king abducted Alexander III from Loch Leven. In 1301 the English attacked but failed to capture it. The Douglases began their long tenure as lairds of the castle in the 14th century, towards the end of which they erected the first and best preserved of the surviving buildings. This was the keep, a rectangular five-storey structure with walls 5 ft (1·5 m) thick. During the next century the island was girdled with a curtain wall, which included in one angle a round tower designed for defence by firearms; within the enclosure were a kitchen, hall and other domestic buildings, but these have vanished without trace.

The castle's island site and geographical situation (near, but not too near, Edinburgh) made it useful as a state prison, and the laird served as gaoler on a number of occasions during the 15th and 16th centuries. Easily the most famous of involuntary guests was Mary, Queen of Scots, who was incarcerated in the round tower after her defeat in June 1567 by the Protestant lords. During the following months she managed to win over the laird's brother and his young orphan cousin, Willy Douglas, who organized her audacious escape on 2 May 1568 – a coup of questionable benefit, since it launched Mary on a final adventure that led to defeat, imprisonment in England, and the headsman's block.

A quarter of a mile (0.5 km) east of
Kinross, 15 miles (24 km) south of
Perth, on the M90 (map page 63)

◆

LUDLOW CASTLE SHROPSHIRE

This very big, well-preserved castle stands on the banks of the River Teme, its landward gates opening directly on to the thriving little town of Ludlow. It remained a centre of power for an unusually long time, used first as a fortress on the Welsh border and later as the administrative head-quarters for Wales and the Marches. However, Ludlow Castle originated in the late 11th century as a small, tight stronghold – a roughly oval walled enclosure, defended by four square mural towers and a large rectangular gatehouse. A deep, rock-cut ditch on the vulnerable town side offered further protection and supplied the necessary building materials. In the following century the gatehouse was heightened and walled up to convert it into a keep, and new curtain walls created a second, very large enclosure or outer bailey. As a result, Ludlow extended over a great oblong area, with the earlier enclosure (inner bailey) tucked away behind its ditch in the north-west corner; and this layout remains essentially unchanged, although about a third of the outer bailey is closed, having become a private garden.

Because the castle remained in use for so long, the inner bailey buildings date from widely different periods. They include a round 12th-century chapel, a great hall and kitchens put up in the 13th century, and two 14th-century blocks of apartments. Ludlow Castle eventually passed to the Dukes of York, serving as a Yorkist stronghold in the Wars of the Roses; a tower at Ludlow is traditionally said to have been the home of Edward IV's little sons before they were taken to perish in the TOWER OF LONDON. Under the Tudors and Stuarts, Ludlow Castle became the headquarters of the Lord President of the Council of the Marches of Wales, several important buildings being added during the Elizabethan period to accommodate officials and magistrates. The castle deteriorated after the abolition of the Council in 1689, until rescued by the Earls of Powis, who still own it. On one celebrated occasion in 1634 the poet John Milton's masque *Comus* was performed here with splendid pageantry; now, appropriately, the castle houses the annual Ludlow Festival.

In the town, 24 miles (38 km)
north of Hereford, on the A49
(map pages 60–1)

◆

The great hall and chapel at Ludlow Castle, viewed from the south-west

MIDDLEHAM CASTLE NORTH YORKSHIRE

Despite its ruinous condition, Middleham is a powerful and impressive castle, with one of the largest keeps in the country; and three different major phases of building are represented on the one site. Earl Alan the Red was the first post-Conquest lord of the area; he built in stone at RICHMOND, only a few miles to the north, but contented himself with putting up a timber castle at Middleham, where its earthwork remains stand some 500 yards (450 m) south-west of the stone castle. This was begun in about 1170 by Robert Fitz Ralph, who built the massive rectangular hall keep, two storeys high and 105 × 78 ft (32 × 24 m) in plan. A forebuilding and stairs (both now vanished) led to the entrance at the east end of the first floor, which was divided by a central wall; on one side of it lay the great hall, pantry and buttery, while the other (west) side was occupied by a great chamber and a smaller family room. The kitchen and stores took up the ground floor, and there were two wells in the vaulted basement.

In the late 13th century, the keep and inner bailey were enclosed by a rectangular wall with towers. This was much altered in the 14th and 15th centuries, during which Middleham's lords also installed a strong gatehouse and additional domestic buildings. The result was to create an up-to-date, quadrangular courtyard castle, of a kind normally built on a virgin site; but the dominating presence of the keep within the courtyard was a curious anomaly, all the harder to explain in that it cramped the new domestic buildings. Although ruinous, the keep, walls and gatehouse have survived, unlike the outer bailey and curtain wall. The extent of the late medieval building carried out by its owners, the Nevilles, was a visible sign of the family's status as great northern magnates. After the defeat and death of Richard Neville, Earl of Warwick and 'Kingmaker', in 1471, Middleham passed to the Crown and entered a slow decline that was brutally accelerated by the rigours of the Civil War.

In the town, 19 miles (30.5 km) north-west of Ripon, on the A6108 (map page 62)

Norham Castle, dating from about 1157

NORHAM CASTLE NORTHUMBERLAND

Standing high, tree-girt and ruinous above the River Tweed, Norham Castle still has the air of romantic grandeur that made it one of the favourite subjects of Britain's greatest painter, J.M.W. Turner. But for its Norman founders the site was only incidentally picturesque: more important considerations were the excellent natural defences offered by the river banks and a ravine on its east side. For most of its active history Norham was the most northerly stronghold of the Bishops of Durham, who exercised almost royal powers over a large area of north-east England in return for guarding the borders against the Scots. Consequently, Norham witnessed many historic events, treaties and trials as well as sieges and sorties.

From about 1157 Bishop Hugh de Puisset built a stone keep and curtain walls here to replace the timber motte-and-bailey castle put up some 30 years earlier. The unusually spacious baileys were necessary to accommodate the impedimenta and following of a great ecclesiastic, and an episcopal palace was built in the north-east corner of the inner bailey. Now, however, the most substantial remains are those of the keep, a huge, square, crumbling mass of red sandstone that still stands about 90 ft (27 m) high – roughly its original three storeys, before it was heightened in the 15th century. Norham's defensive record was exceptional throughout the Middle Ages, and in the early 14th century it twice withstood prolonged sieges by Robert the Bruce's forces. Such episodes made extensive repairs and rebuilding necessary over the centuries; the final occasion was after its temporary capture by the Scots in 1513, when Henry VIII ordered it to be re-equipped with artillery defences. It was half-heartedly kept up during Elizabeth I's reign, but was thereafter left to the mercy of the weather and eager quarrymen.

8 miles (13 km) south-west of Berwick-upon-Tweed, via the A698 and B6470
(map page 62)

◆

NORWICH CASTLE NORFOLK

Although the vast bulk of its keep dominates the city, Norwich Castle has suffered greatly over the centuries. The baileys and any outworks that may have existed have entirely disappeared. The keep itself has been gutted and refloored at different levels from those of the two-storey medieval building. And even the exterior has been refaced – a still recent-looking operation carried out in 1834 by the Victorian architect Anthony Salvin, who substituted British Bath stone for the original Caen stone imported from Normandy. Nevertheless, the outside of Norwich Castle alone is worth the trouble of a visit, since the keep is one of the largest in England, and Salvin and others appear to have respected its original design. This is something to be thankful for, since the outer walls are crowded with an unexpected abundance of low-relief decoration, featuring rows of admirable arcading laid out neatly between pilaster strips and turrets. The large upper-floor windows were another amenity, a little dubious from a military point of view, although they could be fairly effectively defended by the troops inside, who were able to deploy quickly thanks to a gallery cut in the thickness of the wall that ran all the way round the interior.

The first castle on the spot, a timber motte-and-bailey structure, was erected soon after the Conquest; in typically ruthless Norman fashion, 113 houses were demolished to make way for it, and local people were forcibly recruited to work on it. Building in stone began in the 12th century or perhaps even a little earlier, and Norwich Castle was held for the king by a series of constables including the Bigods, whose East Anglian power base frequently tempted them to defy rather than serve the Crown. After a turbulent career under Henry II (1154–89) and King John (1199–1216), Norwich Castle was abruptly retired in 1220, serving as a prison for the next 650 years. Since 1887 it has been part of Norwich's excellent principal museum.

In the centre of the city, off the A140
(map page 61)

◆

NUNNEY CASTLE SOMERSET

Tall and sturdy, yet so compact as to seem almost cramped, Nunney is an unusual castle whose debt to the French style of fortress architecture would be even clearer if its towers still wore their original high-coned caps. Nunney's builder was Sir John de la Mare, who evidently brought back both money and ideas from his service in the French wars. The castle was a brand-new one, and de la Mare could find no better unoccupied spot for it on his native manor than the valley bottom below the village of Nunney – a curious siting for a traditionally high-raised edifice. He was granted a royal licence in 1373, and at about that time built a rectangular four-storey tower house with a moat, surrounded on three sides (the fourth was the local stream) by a now-vanished curtain wall. The tower house makes the impression it does because it occupies a relatively modest space, about 60 × 40 ft (18 × 12 m), and yet has been provided with four huge corner towers, each 30 ft (9 m) in diameter; their cramping effect is most obvious on the two short sides, where only a narrow strip of wall separates the towers.

Although display may well have been a more important

Nunney Castle, built by Sir John de la Mare in about 1373

consideration than any serious military function, defence does take priority in certain respects, notably the paucity of openings on the lower floors; the lord, in his large-windowed hall or chamber on the second and third floors, lived a much brighter life than his servants and retainers on the floors below. The machicolations running the full course round the top of the castle were a French feature, effective but also highly decorative. Hidden away from the great world, Nunney led a peaceful existence until September 1645, when Parliament's cannon smashed the north wall, compelling the castle's rapid surrender and condemning it to become a ruin.

11 miles (17.5 km) east of Shepton
Mallet, off the A361 (map pages 60–1)

OLD WARDOUR CASTLE WILTSHIRE

The history of Old Wardour represents a miniature study in the development of English taste between the 14th and 18th centuries; for it has been successively a fortress-residence, a classicized mansion with a lingering martial air, and a grand romantic ruin in a setting of artfully contrived

Old Wardour Castle, begun in 1393

picturesqueness. It was begun in 1393 for John, 5th Lord Lovel, one of those veterans of the French wars who were responsible for so much late medieval English building. The design of his massive tower house was a curious hybrid: five sides of a hexagon built round a courtyard, with a sixth 'side' consisting of a rectangular block. This block served as a kind of keep-gatehouse, with two towers flanking the entrance and the great hall on the first floor above it and rising through all three storeys of the building; the larger hexagonal area, with floors on each storey, provided the ample, conspicuously luxurious accommodation and conveniently located services that were undoubtedly Lovel's main objective.

But although some of Old Wardour's military features – its machicolations and now-vanished turrets – may have been present for the sake of show or convention, the absence of large windows on the ground floor suggests that some possible defensive role was envisaged for the castle. This had certainly ceased to be so by 1570, when Sir Matthew Arundell employed Robert Smythson, the principal Elizabethan architect, to reconstruct Old Wardour, installing large windows and classicizing many features. The two Civil War sieges and the subsequent slighting of the castle were decisive: the Arundells abandoned it and in the 18th century built a new Wardour Castle nearby. The parkland around 'Old' Wardour was landscaped and, with the addition of a Gothick pavilion and grotto, the castle became a place where ladies and gentlemen could stroll about and muse agreeably on time and change.

14 miles (22.5 km) south-west of
Salisbury, off the A30 (map pages 60–1)

ORFORD CASTLE SUFFOLK

Built on a previously unfortified site, Orford Castle was intended by Henry II to guard the town – at that time a busy port – and also to hold in check the turbulent Bigod

Right The splendid keep at Orford Castle

Earls of Norfolk. With a nice sense of irony, the King effectively financed most of the work by collecting a £1000 fine from Hugh Bigod, who had to pay if he wished to recover his confiscated properties. The keep at Orford was begun in the same year – 1165 – and completed with exceptional speed in 1167; the rest of the defences were in place by 1173. Thanks to Henry II's administrative efficiency, Orford is the first English castle whose construction is documented. Consequently, we know that it cost the exceptionally large sum of £1413 9s 2d, and that the work was supervised by Alnoth, the Keeper of the King's Houses. All traces of the bailey defences have vanished except for the earthworks, but the 90 ft (27 m) keep is both well preserved and unique in its design.

In plan Orford is a polygon with 18 faces – to all intents and purposes a circle, and presumably meant to enjoy the advantages of a round tower, which was harder to undermine and offered a clearer field of fire than a rectangular one. But this presumption is contradicted by the other features of the keep, notably the three huge rectangular towers that buttress and rise above the walls, along with the rectangular forebuilding so neatly fitted into one of the angles between the south tower and the main wall. On the other hand, these extras did help to make the accommodation at Orford truly regal in dimensions. Two of the three storeys are residential, with many comforts that were sophisticated by 12th-century standards, including fireplaces, lavatories and a number of small tower rooms offering unusual privacy. As intended, Orford withstood the Bigods when they rebelled in 1174, but its subsequent history was chequered until it became effectively obsolete in the 14th century.

12 miles (19 km) east of Woodbridge,
on the B1084 (map page 61)

PEMBROKE CASTLE DYFED

In its day Pembroke was the mightiest castle ever built in Wales; and it is still an awe-inspiring sight. Norman penetration along the south coast brought Arnulph de

Pembroke Castle, created by William Marshal

Montgomery here as early as 1093, and it was he who selected Pembroke's site, on a great hump of rock thrusting out into the river, with sheer cliffs falling away on three sides. The present castle, however, is the creation of a famous soldier-statesman, William Marshal, Earl of Pembroke.

Beginning in about 1200, Marshal put up a curtain wall across the headland, and built behind it a huge round keep about 75 ft (23 m) high. Magnates in England were slow to adopt the round tower keep, despite its acknowledged military advantages, but William, holding down hostile territory, chose the most modern, effective and monumental style. The result is even more impressive at close quarters, with 20 ft (6 m) thick walls at the base of the keep and a stone dome, still intact, for its roof. Somewhat later, the castle area was greatly extended when an outer curtain wall was constructed with new and even more advanced features: five round mural towers and a double-towered gatehouse protected by a barbican.

For two centuries and more Pembroke Castle guarded the route to Ireland and played host to monarchs and ministers. But although the future King Henry VII – the final victor in the Wars of the Roses – was born within its walls, the castle saw little action until the 17th-century Civil War. An ambitious mayor, John Poyer, successfully held the town and castle for Parliament, only to change sides inopportunely in 1648, when Oliver Cromwell himself arrived to command the ensuing siege. Since the Parliamentary forces lacked heavy artillery, Pembroke's massive walls proved every bit as effective as they had been in the Middle Ages. Attempts at direct assault were repulsed, and it was seven weeks before the defenders were starved, or possibly parched, into surrender; according to local belief, resistance only ended after a traitor revealed the whereabouts of the water supply to the besiegers. The subsequent slighting of Pembroke Castle was proportionately harsh, and the apparently excellent state of the curtain towers and gatehouse is in fact a tribute to the skills of their 20th-century restorers.

On the west side of the town, off the
A477 (map page 60)

PEVENSEY CASTLE   EAST SUSSEX

Although now inland, Pevensey stood at a strategic spot on the south coast until the late Middle Ages. That is why the Romans chose it as the site of Anderida, a large (eight-acre) fort designed to protect 'the Saxon Shore' (that is, the coastline threatened by Saxon raids). It was abandoned in the 5th century, but William the Conqueror landed at Pevensey in 1066 and immediately put up a castle – possibly brought over, prefabricated, from Normandy – inside the walls of the old fort. William soon moved on to Hastings, but after the Conquest his half-brother, Robert de Mortain, followed his leader's example. He built a hall or keep, surrounded by a palisade and ditch, in the south-west corner of Anderida, thus turning the rest of the Roman fort into a sort of huge outer bailey.

After a turbulent history as a baronial castle, Pevensey passed to Henry II (1154–89), who built the present keep and (probably) the three rather odd, rounded buttresses that project strongly from its east and west sides. In the 13th century, defences were brought up to date when the inner bailey was provided with a curtain wall, three 'D'-shaped mural towers and a twin-towered gatehouse. The silting up of the coastline made Pevensey Castle obsolete, and from the 15th century it was allowed to decay; but although the keep and gatehouse are very broken down, much else – including Roman walling – has survived, and the basic layout is easily identified. During World War II camouflaged defences were installed at Pevensey to combat a possible German invasion; and when peace broke out somebody took the imaginative decision to leave machine-gun posts in place, so that the visitor can now find evidence of a military role at the site over some 1700 years.

5 miles (8 km) north-east of
Eastbourne, on the A259 (map page 61)

PORTCHESTER CASTLE   HAMPSHIRE

Portchester Castle, like PEVENSEY (East Sussex), began as a Roman fort, was eventually abandoned, and was re-occupied centuries later by the Normans, who built a castle with a curtain wall in one corner of the site. The rest of the fort became a huge outer bailey – and a deeply impressive one, since the site comprised a very large, regular square, encompassed by walls that were (and still are) 20 ft (6 m) high and 10 ft (3 m) thick, with strong, closely spaced mural towers guarding them. The only Norman additions here are two entrances (each a rectangular tower with a passageway through it) positioned midway along the east and west walls.

The relatively modest rectangular inner bailey consisted initially of a two-storey keep, curtain walls, a square corner tower and a gatehouse, all dating from the early 12th century; a few decades later, the keep was heightened by two storeys and the barbican was constructed. Finally, in the 14th century, ranges of domestic buildings were built in the area between the keep and the gatehouse. All of these, although ruinous, are still standing, so there is much to be seen at Portchester, including the church in the far south-eastern corner, which is all that now survives of the Augustinian priory founded there.

From the reign of Henry II (1154–89) Portchester was a royal castle, frequently used as an assembly point for armies bound for France. But with the rise of nearby Portsmouth and changes in fortification techniques its usefulness

rapidly declined during the 15th century, and its later career as an occasional barracks or prison was unheroic.

In the town, 3 miles (5 km) east of
Fareham, on the A27 (map page 61)

RABY CASTLE   COUNTY DURHAM

With its sprawling array of towers, walls and battlements rising above a neat, relatively low outer curtain wall, Raby is intended to impress, and does so very effectively. For two centuries it was the chief stronghold of a great northern family, the Nevilles, who became Earls of Westmorland from 1397 – and the only dangerous rivals of the Percy 'kings' of the North. A royal licence was issued to John, Lord Neville, in 1378, and he built Raby as a counterpart to the great Percy castle at ALNWICK (Northumberland). Subsequent building and rebuilding has made the castle a complicated and irregular structure, but there is still a rectangular court at its heart, and the siting of four out of the five towers suggests that Raby may originally have been built on a conventional quadrangular plan. It has been argued that the fifth tower (Clifford's Tower) was originally a separate unit, possibly a keep-like residence for the lord; and the fact that the tower commands the outer gateway makes this even more plausible.

It is not certain whether Raby was ever very effective as a fortress, but the wealth of buildings, the emphatic, unfunctional crenellation and the heraldic displays indicate that its most important purpose was to make manifest the greatness of the Nevilles. This was sustained throughout the 15th century, but began to falter under the Tudors; and when the Nevilles backed the Catholic rising of 1569 against Elizabeth I, their fall was swift and complete. Raby remained Crown property until Sir Henry Vane bought it in 1626, and his prominence on the Parliamentary side in the Civil War meant that there was no question of it being slighted. Major alterations in the 18th and 19th centuries turned the castle

Portchester Castle has a church at its south-eastern corner

into a country house, replete with lavish interiors and *objets d'art*, but the spacious, vaulted medieval kitchens survive as one of its most uncommon attractions.

**6 miles (9.5 km) north-east of Barnard
Castle at Stairdrop, on the A688
(map page 62)**

◆

RAGLAN CASTLE GWENT

This noble ruin testifies to the continuing importance of the castle in 15th-century Britain, especially as an expression of rapid upward mobility. Raglan was begun in about 1435 by Sir William ap Thomas, who had married and administered his way to great wealth; but the greater part of it was built by his son, Sir William Herbert, an outstanding Yorkist leader in the Wars of the Roses whose services were eventually rewarded with the earldom of Pembroke. Both father and son had fought in the French wars, and there is a distinctly Continental air about Raglan's most striking feature – the six-sided tower keep, fully independent within its own moat and equipped with kitchen, hall, private apartments and bedrooms.

The rest of the castle is entered by a fine machicolated, twin-towered gatehouse, and consists essentially of ranges of buildings and towers laid out in a rectangle; this is divided into two courts (the Fountain Court and the Pitched Stone Court) by the great hall built across it. The accommodation at Raglan was therefore lavish, and a Welsh poet sang in praise of its 'hundred rooms full of festive fare'. But it was also intended as a fighting castle, with plenty of gunports to indicate that the garrison meant business. The tower keep is presumed to have functioned as the lord's private apartments and also as a place of last resort in an emergency; the gunports of the keep point not only outwards but also, ominously, in towards the castle buildings.

Unluckily for William Herbert, he was not besieged at Raglan when the Lancastrians made a comeback in 1469,

Left Raby Castle, built by Lord Neville in 1378

The twin-towered gatehouse of Raglan Castle

but captured after a battle in the open field and executed immediately. Raglan's high heroic moment came in 1646, when the aged Earl of Warwick held out in the castle against Parliament from June to August. The gallant defenders were allowed to march out with flying colours, but the subsequent slighting of Raglan ended its career.

**7 miles (11 km) south-west of
Monmouth, on the A40 (map page 60)**

◆

RESTORMEL CASTLE CORNWALL

Satisfyingly round, well proportioned and spacious, the shell keep at Restormel is probably the outstanding example of this type of British castle. Its site is a natural hilltop overlooking the River Fowey, falling away steeply on three sides and made still less accessible by an extremely wide man-made ditch. The fourth, western side of the hill must have contained the castle bailey, but no trace of this remains. There was an earlier castle of some sort here, but by about 1200 it had been replaced by the present stone shell – a round curtain wall with a big square gatehouse to the south-west and, on the opposite side of the curtain, a chapel tower projecting beyond the wall.

Like other castles in the county, Restormel benefited from the fact that Cornwall was royal property. Its most distinctive features were the work of Henry III's brother, Richard of Cornwall (d. 1271), or, more likely, his son Edmund (d. 1300). One or both of them were responsible for the luxuriously large domestic quarters arranged all the way round the circuit of the walls, leaving a small circular courtyard in the centre of the castle; when viewed from the battlements, the spoke-like symmetry of their roofless walls is very striking. Restormel was probably intended as a grand princely hunting lodge, but its windows were arranged with strict military logic, looking inwards on the inner wall of the ground-floor buildings and outwards only on the upper levels of the shell wall.

Following a period of neglect, Restormel enjoyed another brief heyday when the Black Prince repaired the castle and, as Duke of Cornwall, stayed there in 1354 and 1362. Although the castle saw some fighting during the Civil War, it was already 'utterly ruined' according to a Parliamentary Commission, and so escaped slighting. Overgrown and virtually forgotten for centuries, Restormel was presented to the nation by the Duke of Cornwall in 1925, after which the site was cleared and this very elegant castle was brought back into public view.

1 mile (1.5 km) north of Lostwithiel,
via the B3268 (map page 60)

RHUDDLAN CASTLE   CLWYD

Rhuddlan stands at the lowest crossing-point of the River Clwyd, which for centuries provided a relatively safe route through difficult terrain into North Wales. Before the Conquest, Welsh and Saxon princes fought to control it, and in 1073 a Norman noble, Robert of Rhuddlan, built a motte-and-bailey castle close to the river, where its mound can still be seen.

Although the Welsh subsequently recovered the area,

some sort of accommodation was probably still available at the old castle in August 1277, when Edward I moved to Rhuddlan from Chester during his first campaign against Llywelyn ap Gruffydd. Within a few weeks of his arrival, having already ordered the building of a castle at Flint, Edward began work on a second one at Rhuddlan, just north-west of the Norman motte. By 1284, when war broke out again, the castle was sufficiently strong for the King to make it his headquarters, and it was from Rhuddlan that the famous Statute, dividing North Wales into English-style shires, was issued.

An early British work by Master James of St George, Rhuddlan is a fine example of a concentric castle; the outer curtain is very broken down, but the inner ward remains an impressive sight, a near-square area with high curtain walls, two massive twin-towered gatehouses at diagonally opposite angles, and sturdy round towers at the other angles.

The greatest feat was performed by 1800 imported ditchers, who dug out the three sides of the castle's moat and carved out a canal on the fourth side to bring the Clwyd – and, potentially, relief from the sea – right up to the walls. The effectiveness of this precaution was demonstrated in 1294 and again in 1400, when Welsh rebels failed to capture Rhuddlan Castle. As a Royalist stronghold during the Civil War, the castle was ordered to undergo a 'demolishment' that was carried out with deplorable energy.

South-west of the town, 12 miles
(19 km) east of Colwyn Bay, via the A55
and A547 (map page 62)

ROCHESTER CASTLE   KENT

Rochester controls the crossing-point of the River Medway on the London to Dover road, and the Normans quickly grasped its strategic importance. A timber castle went up here soon after the Conquest, and at a very early date – about 1088 – Bishop Gundulf of Rochester replaced it with a new castle in stone, consisting of a curtain wall round an enclosure. Some stretches of this and later outer

Continued on page 136

Rhuddlan Castle was built by Master James of St George for Edward I

Guided Tour

RICHMOND CASTLE
NORTH YORKSHIRE

Richmond is still recognizably the castle erected within a few years of the Norman Conquest by Alan the Red, a Breton follower of King William. He built on a triangular platform whose south side, high above the River Swale, required little in the way of defence; so he put up walls with towers on the other two sides of the triangle, which became the Great Court, and placed the principal entrance, suitably defended, at its apex. Later building on the site merely elaborated on this simple, sensible arrangement, or made the castle a more comfortable place in which to live.

Today you can walk from the thriving little town of Richmond into the barbican area of the castle. Its outer gatehouse and most of the original masonry have disappeared, and what now commands the attention is the 100 ft (30 m) high compact mass of the keep, looming up on the right, with its pilaster strips patterning the surface in low relief, and its three ecclesiastical-looking arched windows. The keep is reached by walking through a modern entrance block into the Great Court and turning into an impressive ground-floor archway. This was part of the original Norman gatehouse built by Earl Alan, but was filled in and incorporated into the keep which replaced it in the late 12th century. As usual, the original entrance to the keep was on the first floor; it still exists, nowadays linked to the Great Court by a platform and set of steps. The first floor is reached by a spiral staircase, after which two sets of steps, dramatically built into the thickness of the wall, lead right up to the battlements, which offer splendid views.

The steps from the keep's first-floor entrance go down to the east curtain wall. Further along stands Robin Hood Tower, in which the Scottish king William the Lion is said to have been imprisoned. Its ground floor was a chapel, with dignified low-relief arcading on the walls and a window whose flat sill probably supported the altar table. Beyond a very ruinous group of residential buildings (a chapel and 'Great Chamber') stands Scolland's Hall fronting the river. Named after Earl Alan's steward, this is one of the few surviving examples of an early post-Conquest hall. Now a shell, open to the sky, it too was originally entered at first-floor level, up stone steps whose broken base still stands on the green. Earl Alan could retire directly from the hall into his solar or private chamber, but now this is reached via the Great Court and Great Chamber. Standing today in the solar and looking down on the hall brings home the comparatively confined nature of domestic life at that time, even as lived by a great Norman lord.

Back on the ground, an arched entry under the solar leads into the Cockpit, a lesser court or bailey that was enclosed in the 12th century. To the left stands the well-preserved and entertainingly named Gold Hole Tower, which was the 11th-century latrine block. On the river front, adjoining Scolland's Hall, are the ruins of the kitchen and service areas; beyond this, the remains are low and fragmentary, making it possible to appreciate the view of the Swale and the steepness with which the ground slopes away to it. A tower guards the angle at which the river front meets the west curtain wall, which consists mainly of 11th-century masonry that stretches as far as the discreet modern latrine block. A wide, open arch in the wall at first-floor level represents the west end of the castle's great chapel, with a postern gate below it. Following the line of the west curtain brings the visitor back to the keep and the main entrance.

Paradoxically, this once-great Norman stronghold was too remote from the main centres of power to play much part in the national history. Neglect, not siege warfare, reduced it to the 'mere ruin' that a visitor found in 1540.

In the town, 13 miles (21 km) south-west of Darlington, via the M1 and A6108 (map page 62)

Right Situated high above the River Swale, Richmond Castle had a surprisingly uneventful history

ROBIN HOOD TOWER

GOLD HOLE TOWER

SCOLLAND'S HALL

Rochester Castle, built in about 1088

Continued from page 132

defences have survived, but for most people the focus of interest at Rochester is the magnificent keep erected between about 1127 and 1140 by another ecclesiastic, William de Corbeil, Archbishop of Canterbury.

The keep is both massive and high – at 125 ft (38 m) the tallest in England, with four corner towers and an impressive rectangular forebuilding housing the entrance; at ground-floor level the walls are a daunting 12 ft (3.5 m) thick. Inside, the roof and floors have gone, but it is still possible to appreciate the staircases in the thickness of the wall spiralling to the battlements, and the strong cross-wall neatly dividing the accommodation into two equal parts. There were four storeys, with the principal apartments on the second floor rising through two levels; here the cross-wall was pierced with round arches, becoming an elegant arcaded partition. With such spacious accommodation, two chapels, a well, privies, and even a dovecote on the battlements, Rochester Castle was a place where the lord could lead a full life even when surrounded by enemies.

One major alteration was made after the famous siege of 1215, at which King John's men succeeded in undermining and bringing down the south-east corner: John's successor, Henry III, restored the corner after the fashion of the day, with a round tower, despite its incongruity *vis-à-vis* the three earlier, rectangular towers. Now Crown property, Rochester was besieged again in 1264 by Simon de Montfort, but relieved by a Royalist army. Although the damage was eventually made good by Edward III and Richard II, in the 15th century the castle was abandoned.

In the town, 8 miles (13 km) north of Maidstone, on the A229 (map page 61)

ROCKINGHAM CASTLE   NORTHAMPTONSHIRE

The approach to Rockingham Castle is somewhat misleading, since its two tremendous entrance towers are easily its most martial features; within, its main character is that of a Tudor mansion, although one that is superimposed on much earlier fabric, and has been altered and augmented in more recent times. Rockingham stands high on a hill, and was a fortified place even in Anglo-Saxon times. After the Norman Conquest, King William built a timber motte-and-bailey castle here which was later converted to stone, and Rockingham was frequently visited by its royal owners, perhaps for the good hunting in the forests just below. Now, however, the most important medieval remains are those of improvements made in the 13th century – above all the great gatehouse put up by Edward I, with drum towers so wide that despite their height they give the impression of being squat.

Part of the outer curtain wall is 13th-century, and so is the great hall now so tamed and Tudored. Its rebuilding was the work of Edward Watson, who in 1530 took over a dilapidated castle that had been neglected by its royal owners, and turned it into a Tudor mansion. The changes over the next few centuries epitomized one aspect of social and architectural history: for example, the hall – a symbol of feudal state – was divided into two rooms and its ceiling was lowered; but in the 17th century a grand long gallery provided the family in residence with ample space for their private leisure pursuits. There was further building at Rockingham over the centuries, including some by the ubiquitous Victorian 'creative restorer', Anthony Salvin. The Watson family still owns the castle, which contains many objects of historical interest and fine paintings, as well as being set in 12 acres of lovely gardens, both formal and wild.

2 miles (3 km) north of Corby, on the
A6003 (map page 61)

ROTHESAY CASTLE   STRATHCLYDE

This unusual castle stands on the island of Bute, just off the west coast of Scotland – territory disputed between the Norse and Scottish kings as late as the 13th century. The castle dates back to the 12th century and took the form of a circular curtain wall surrounded by a wide moat. According to one of the sagas, the siege of 1230 by Uspek and his Norsemen showed up the weakness of Rothesay, since the besiegers managed to break right through the wall. It was probably in response to this that four huge drum towers, some 35 ft (10.5 m) across, were added to the wall; the north-west tower is much the best preserved.

In 1263 Alexander III won a decisive victory at the Battle of Largs that ended the Norse threat. Rothesay became a favoured residence of the Scottish kings, and further improvements were made to the defences at the end of the 15th century. One was to raise the level of the walls by 10 ft (3 m); even now, the outline of the earlier battlements can be picked out. The other was to install a great three-storey gatehouse that thrust right out into the moat, offering increased security and spacious accommodation. It is still well preserved – by contrast with the domestic accommodation in the courtyard, of which only a 16th-century chapel survives.

Rothesay Castle's fortunes were mixed during the Middle Ages, but the 17th century was disastrous: Cromwell's troops are said to have slighted it, and in 1685 it was certainly burned by rebels. The castle was restored in the 19th century by the Marquises of Bute, but in 1961 it passed into the care of the state.

In the town on the island of Bute, via
the A886 (map page 63)

ST MAWES CASTLE   CORNWALL

Small and elegant, St Mawes is perhaps the most visually delightful of the artillery forts built along England's south coast by Henry VIII. It has a non-identical twin in Pendennis Castle, on the other side of the Carrick Roads estuary, over which the two forts could direct a devastating crossfire to repel raiders and invaders bent on attacking Falmouth harbour and the Cornish interior. But whereas Pendennis was enlarged and strengthened during the reign of Elizabeth I, St Mawes remained as it had been after its original construction in 1540–3.

The present-day fort, with its rebuilt watch tower, has therefore much to offer the visitor, most pertinently the skilfully sited embrasures and recesses at all levels, with smoke vents and storage-places for ammunition. There are also many interesting decorative touches, including the set of Latin inscriptions specially devised for St Mawes by the King's antiquary, John Leland.

The actual history of the fort was unexciting and unromantic. King Henry remained secure, and in 1588 the Spanish Armada passed the fort by. Then the Civil War put St Mawes to an unfair test for which it was never designed. In March 1646, helpless against an attack from the land side, it immediately surrendered to Parliament. In spite of this, St Mawes remained part of the coastal defences until the 19th century, and was brought out of retirement to serve in both World Wars.

In the town, 19 miles (30.5 km) south of
Truro, on the A3078 (map page 60)

SCARBOROUGH CASTLE   NORTH YORKSHIRE

The site of Scarborough Castle is a magnificent natural fortress: a triangular headland looking out on the North Sea from a height of 300 ft (90 m) or more. So it is not surprising that the remains here include those of a Roman signal station, in its day a tower about the same size as the keep erected some 750 years later. Between times, in about 1130, William le Gros, Earl of Albemarle and Holderness, took advantage of the disturbed conditions of King Stephen's reign to put up a castle of some sort at Scarborough. Then, in the 1160s, as part of his restoration of order, Henry II dismantled William's adulterine building and proceeded to erect one of his own. Its heart was a powerful keep which is still impressive although reduced to a high, hollow fragment.

However, the most striking feature at Scarborough is the curtain wall with mural towers, built a few decades later (probably by King John), which runs all the way across the headland; in combination with the keep and the powerful barbican, it made an assault on the castle a daunting undertaking. And Scarborough did live up to appearances, successfully weathering a number of sieges. When it was compelled to surrender in 1312, the cause was a combination of lack of food and the specious promises made by its baronial besiegers. In 1645 Parliamentary troops took Scarborough Castle by assault after a bombardment that smashed the keep, and following a further engagement in 1648 its history as a fortress came to an end.

To the east of the town centre, off the A165
(map page 62)

———◆———

SIZERGH CASTLE   CUMBRIA

Two phases of northern English history are mirrored by the buildings at Sizergh: the turbulent time of wild affrays and fearful insecurity, and the subsequent Tudor age of growing wealth and peace that culminated in the union

Left *The ruins of Scarborough Castle*

Sizergh Castle, the result of two main phases of building

of Scottish and English crowns in 1603. The Strickland family moved to Sizergh in 1239, and live there still (now as tenants of the National Trust). In the 1330s, responding to the revival of Anglo-Scottish wars and cross-border raiding, Sir Walter Strickland swept away any buildings already on the site and put up a residential tower strong enough to withstand anything but a full-scale invasion. Many northern families were constructing pele towers of this sort, but Strickland's was one of the biggest, a stolid four-storey rectangle some 60 ft (18 m) high and 60 × 40 ft (18 × 12 m) in plan, with the rectangular Deincourt Tower projecting from the south wall and rising 10 ft (3 m) above it. The pele walls were 9 ft (2.75 m) thick at the base, which would take the brunt of any attack, thinning down to just over half that thickness on the top floor.

The pele itself bears witness to the coming of more tranquil times in the size of its windows, enlarged during the 15th century; but the later buildings are far more elegant. A great hall was erected beside the tower, followed by two wings at right-angles, so that Sizergh now occupies three sides of a courtyard. Its fine interiors and furnishings also date from Tudor or later times, as do those symbols of confidence in the established order – the lovely rock, water and herbaceous gardens of Sizergh.

3½ miles (5.5 km) south of Kendal, off
the A591 (map page 62)

———◆———

SKIPTON CASTLE NORTH YORKSHIRE

This castle is exceptionally well integrated into the busy market town it once dominated, since its outer gatehouse actually stands at the end of the high street. There was a Norman castle on the spot in the 11th century, but the real history of Skipton Castle begins with Robert de Clifford, who rebuilt it before his death at Bannockburn (1314). The Cliffords then had a three-centuries-long run as late medieval magnates, becoming conspicuous for their loyalty to the Crown. As castellans of York they built the city's castle, CLIFFORD'S TOWER, but they resided almost continuously at Skipton except during the period of Yorkist ascendancy during the Wars of the Roses, when their lands and castle were temporarily forfeited. During the Civil War, Skipton was the last Royalist fortress in the North to capitulate, and was slighted by Parliament; but unlike most castles it was repaired before the deterioration of the fabric had gone too far. Skipton's saviour, Lady Anne Clifford, was the last of her line, and by restoring castles and other Clifford buildings she may have hoped to perpetuate the family name; at any rate she had the Clifford motto, *Desormais* ('Hereafter'), placed prominently along the balustrade of Skipton's 14th-century gatehouse, one of the parts of the castle that she restored in 1657–8.

In plan, the heart of the castle is a 'D'-shape, the straight north side being a plain curtain wall along the top of the steep river bank. The curved curtain is defended by six round towers: one at each junction with the straight curtain, two stationed together in the centre to form an inner gatehouse, and one on each side between junction and gatehouse. The charming courtyard, known as the Conduit Court, is a late 15th-century creation, but the range of buildings against the north curtain wall dates from about 1300. To the east of the castle lies a typical Tudor addition of a house that was originally meant to be the castle's long gallery.

In the town, 19 miles (30.5 km) north-west
of Bradford, via the A650 and A629
(map page 62)

Stirling, in former times 'the key to the Highlands'

STIRLING CASTLE CENTRAL

Like its counterpart at EDINBURGH (Lothian), Stirling Castle stands high on a ridge of volcanic rock that falls away towards the town below. For centuries Stirling was the more important of the two castles, controlling the ford across the Forth and the route into the Highlands. None of the present castle buildings predates the 15th century, but it is impossible to ignore Stirling's unseen past, for it was the key to controlling Scotland during the wars of independence; Edward I besieged and captured it in 1304, the Scots recovered it in 1314, and it changed hands again before the English were finally expelled.

Surprisingly, the fortifications down to this time seem to have been mainly of timber. Building in stone on a large scale was carried out by the 15th- and 16th-century Stuart kings, for whom Stirling Castle became a favourite residence. James III and James IV built the great hall, completed in 1503; James IV and James V were responsible for the fine Renaissance palace, importing French masons to execute the fine detail; and in 1594 James VI erected a splendid new royal chapel for the baptism of his son Prince Henry. These remain the principal buildings, somewhat affected by the use of the castle as a barracks and for other military purposes from the 18th century onwards – activities that were also responsible for the later buildings on the site.

When James VI became James I of England in 1603, he and his court moved south and the spate of building at Stirling Castle came to an abrupt end. Monck's English

The entrance to Skipton, a medieval castle restored in the 17th century

Parliamentary army battered and took it in 1651, something that Bonnie Prince Charlie failed to do in 1745. It was used by the military until 1964 (and still houses the headquarters and regimental museum of the Argyll and Sutherland Highlanders), since when much restoration work has been done.

In the town centre, off the M9
(map page 63)

◆

STOKESAY CASTLE   SHROPSHIRE

Stokesay Castle is an extraordinarily picturesque, early and authentic example of a medieval fortified house, designed with an eye to comfort as much as to defence. However, the disappearance of its water defences and curtain wall make it seem less formidable now than was once the case, and this misleading impression is reinforced by the present half-timbered Elizabethan building that serves as a gatehouse. After passing through this the visitor is confronted with a long, large-windowed range of domestic buildings and, to the left, the large, powerful-looking south tower. At the far end of the domestic range, disguised beneath more half-timbering, stands the oldest surviving part of Stokesay, the north tower. This and the hall were already built in 1281, when the property was purchased by a wealthy merchant, Lawrence of Ludlow. He completed the hall and then, having obtained a licence to crenellate in 1291, built the south tower. He also added a private chamber which was not accessible from the hall, but only by a set of outside steps; however, the family could keep an eye on their retainers through one of the 'squint' holes beside the fireplace. The interiors at Stokesay are splendidly atmospheric – especially the private chamber or solar, with its Elizabethan oak panelling and lavishly decorated fireplace, and the lofty, timber-roofed hall.

Given the size of the windows, the castle can never have been intended for prolonged defence, but in times of serious trouble it would always have been possible for the family to take refuge in the south tower. In the event, Lawrence of Ludlow's descendants lived at Stokesay for 300 years with few serious alarms, and their successors, the Cravens, were almost as fortunate. From the 18th century the house was let as a farm or workshop, and these relatively humble functions may well have been the salvation of Stokesay, since they ensured that the house was never modernized out of all recognition. After its sale by the Cravens in 1869, the new owners began restoring it to its present splendid condition.

8 miles (13 km) north-west of Ludlow,
off the A49 (map page 60)

◆

TAMWORTH CASTLE   STAFFORDSHIRE

A sturdy, well-preserved, multi-angled shell keep, Tamworth Castle has stood on its mound overlooking the River Tame since the late 12th century. The mound itself is a century or so older, hinting at the existence of earlier structures, and some Norman masonry in the characteristic herringbone pattern may be contemporary with Robert de Marmion, who as first King's Champion was given the lordship of Tamworth by William the Conqueror. (A more famous Marmion, the hero of Sir Walter Scott's narrative poem, was one of Robert's descendants.) Soon after the building of the shell keep, a somewhat higher square tower was inserted into the wall, protecting the entrance and serving as a stronghold or place of final resort in an emergency.

In the 15th century the Marmions were replaced by the Ferrers family, and at Tamworth defensive considerations gave way to a quest for comfort and display. At this time or later, the bailey was neglected and eventually disappeared altogether. The medieval buildings inside the shell wall were dismantled and replaced over the generations with superior accommodation, although it is possible that the new structures followed the layout of the old. Tamworth's history was uneventful and it was untouched by the Civil War and its aftermath, so although the years have taken their toll, there is much to see. Inside, the great hall is particularly impressive, with bold, ornate, deeply-cut stone panelling and fine carved chimneypieces. The other attractions of the castle include panelled Jacobean rooms, a 'haunted room' and a Norman exhibition.

In the town, 17 miles (27 km) north-
east of Birmingham, on the A453
(map page 61)

English Parliament's General Monck bombarded it in 1651. In 1699 the Earl of Angus sold it to an asset-stripper, after which it was abandoned for good.

2½ miles (4 km) east of North Berwick,
on the A198 (map page 63)

TANTALLON CASTLE   LOTHIAN

Tantallon is one of Scotland's great historic castles, spectacular in setting and still majestic in decay. It stands on a cliff top that thrusts out into the Firth of Forth, in which the Bass Rock is clearly visible some 2 miles (3 km) away. At Tantallon the rock faces fall away steeply to the sea on three sides, so the obvious way of creating a stronghold was to put up a line of defences across a convenient neck of land; and this was done at some time in the late 14th century, possibly by William, the 1st Earl of Douglas. Today the heart of the castle is still protected by the great rock-cut ditch that runs from one side of the cliff to another; and behind it stands a strong wall, 50 ft (15 m) high and 12 ft (3.5 m) thick, with a mighty 80 ft (24 m) high gatehouse in the centre and a tower at each end.

On the north side of the close or courtyard are the remains of a range of domestic buildings, although as usual the gatehouse contained a hall and other residential rooms from which the laird could direct the defence at a time of crisis. Crises were almost ludicrously common in the history of the Douglas family (Earls of Douglas, and later of Angus), which from generation to generation engaged in political intrigues, rebellions and (surprisingly often) treasonable dealings with English monarchs, the result being that hasty retreats to Tantallon were also common.

The castle withstood a royal siege in 1491, but fell – by negotiation rather than storm – in 1528. However, James V's cannon had done damage, and the King proceeded to strengthen the gatehouse against artillery – a precaution from which the Earl of Angus benefited when he returned from exile and claimed back Tantallon. The castle suffered during the turbulent 17th century, especially when the

TATTERSHALL CASTLE   LINCOLNSHIRE

A red-brick colossus looming above the flat Lincolnshire landscape, the great tower keep at Tattershall was built in the 1430s by Ralph Cromwell, Lord Treasurer of England. It is the sole survivor of a much more extensive castle which Cromwell added to the relatively modest family residence in celebration of his rise to eminence, and perhaps to provide himself with a secure base. With its pioneering use of brick, decorative façades, hexagonal turrets and great height of 110 ft (33 m), the tower was undoubtedly intended to impress; but experts have never

The tower keep of Tattershall Castle

Thirlestane Castle is the result of three major building phases: 1590, 1670 and 1840

been in full agreement concerning its military role.

Features such as the use of brick (which is hardly artillery-proof), and also the installation of large, light-welcoming but vulnerable windows on the ground floor, suggest that fashion and comfort were more important to Cromwell than defensive considerations; on the other hand, the tower's machicolations are functional as well as decorative, and research has shown that the castle as a whole was laid out on approved military lines. In spite of this, Tattershall was not involved in the dynastic and civil troubles of the next two centuries, although it was nevertheless abandoned and allowed to fall into ruin.

A last-minute rescue was effected by Lord Curzon, the former Viceroy of India, who bought the castle in 1911 and restored it lovingly and thoroughly. He also recovered its finest internal features – four splendid carved stone chimney-pieces which had been taken out and sold to American buyers. This was all the more satisfying since Cromwell had obviously intended them to be significant parts of his proud self-display. They carry not only the heraldic shields of the Lord Treasurer and his wife, but also an apt symbol of his office – a purse, elegant, tasselled, and presumably full.

9 miles (14.5 km) south of Horncastle,
on the A153 (map pages 61–2)

◆

THIRLESTANE CASTLE   BORDERS

Encapsulating centuries of social change, Thirlestane began as a 16th-century castle, was transformed a century later into a Renaissance-style palace, and was finally enlarged to make a Victorian stately home. During this entire period it was the home of the Maitland family, whose head was Earl (and in a single case Duke) of Lauderdale. The nucleus of the present building was the castle built in 1590, an oblong structure with a round tower at each corner.

The next major phase of building was initiated by John Maitland, Duke of Lauderdale, who ruled Scotland with autocratic rigour on behalf of Charles II. As at his other residences, he employed the classicizing Scottish architect Sir William Bruce, who in 1670 remodelled Thirlestane on approved Renaissance lines, giving it a symmetrical main (west) façade. The interiors were likewise reconstructed according to the taste of the time, but the main surviving glories of the castle were probably the work of Charles II's 'gentleman modeller', George Dunsterfield; these are the plasterwork ceilings with splendidly moulded garlands and clusters of leaves, flowers and fruit.

In 1840 the architect David Bryce carried out new work at Thirlestane, but he treated Bruce's design with a certain sensitivity, extending the main façade but maintaining its classical symmetry. However, his tower-cappings – in particular the large ogee caps he added to the central tower – rather altered the mood of the building, giving it a faintly oriental air that is far from disagreeable. Notable among the interesting exhibits at Thirlestane is a huge collection of children's toys of the past.

At Lauder, 26 miles (42 km)
south-east of Edinburgh, on the A68
(map page 62)

◆

THREAVE CASTLE   DUMFRIES AND GALLOWAY

Viewed across the waters of the Dee, Threave Castle is a heart-stirring sight. The surroundings that make it so bleakly romantic also served as its first line of defence, for the castle stands on a grassy island in the river, commanding the only ford. It became the great stronghold of the Black Douglases, who for hundreds of years played a leading role in the turbulent history of Scotland. The tower house at Threave was built by one of the most successful members of the family, Archibald the Grim, 3rd Earl of Douglas, whose lifetime of action and intrigue brought him wealth, power and also enhanced status: he achieved the ultimate ambition of any feudal lord, marrying his children into the Scottish royal family. Archibald's tower house was a sturdy five-storey oblong block that still stands to about 70 ft (21 m) despite its ruinous condition. Now its most distinctive feature is the triple row of holes just below the

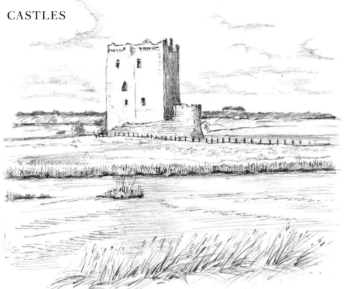

Threave Castle, situated on an island in the River Dee

roof line, which presumably held the joists of a wooden fighting gallery.

In about the mid 15th century, the defences were greatly strengthened by the erection of a rectangular outer curtain wall with a gatehouse and round corner towers (only one of which survives), well provided with gunports. It is not clear whether this was done before or after the siege of 1454 in which Threave was bombarded by James II as part of his successful campaign to break the Douglas power. The castle eventually passed to the Maxwell Earls of Nithsdale, who held it until 1640, when the Covenanters seized it from the Royalist 3rd Earl and made a thorough job of stripping and disabling it. After this, Threave was only used once more, to hold prisoners during the Napoleonic wars.

1 mile (1.5 km) west of Castle Douglas,
off the A75 (map page 62)

◆

TINTAGEL CASTLE   CORNWALL

There is no more romantic ruin in the country than Tintagel Castle, although it must be admitted that the pleasures it offers are mainly aesthetic and imaginative. In this rugged, spectacularly storm-lashed place, the castle sprawls down a rocky headland and then continues on the cliffs of the island just beyond it. The two parts are now linked by a bridge, but in the Middle Ages the only way across was a causeway which, according to the chronicler Geoffrey of Monmouth, could accommodate no more than three men abreast.

Tintagel owes much of its glamour and atmosphere to Geoffrey, for it was he who first recorded – or invented – the legend that King Arthur was conceived in the castle. Geoffrey's *History of the Kings of Britain* (*c.* 1136) describes how King Uther Pendragon fell in love with Ygerna, wife of the Duke of Cornwall, and, using one of Merlin's spells to turn himself into the Duke's double, was able to gain admittance to the castle and spend that momentous, Arthur-making night with the unwitting Ygerna.

Unfortunately, although Geoffrey accurately describes Tintagel's island site, there is no evidence of a castle there until after his book was finished. The first builder was Reginald, Earl of Cornwall, the remains of whose great hall (*c.* 1145) can still be seen on the island. A century later, the energetic and ambitious Richard of Cornwall worked on a grander scale, putting up the curtain wall around the inner (island) ward and creating the two extensive wards on the mainland. Despite some 14th-century rebuilding, Tintagel's remoteness soon began to tell against it, and by the 15th century it had been abandoned to the elements.

6 miles (9.5 km) north-west of
Camelford, via the B3266 and B3263
(map page 60)

◆

TOWER OF LONDON   LONDON

The Tower of London is notoriously associated with dark deeds: it is the place where the 'little princes' were done away with, the state prison from which few ever emerged, and the site of many executions. And at the same time it is a colourful 'heritage' attraction, featuring collections of arms and armour, prisoners' graffiti, instruments of torture, 'Beefeaters' (Yeoman Warders), ravens, the Crown Jewels and the coronation regalia. All this makes it easy to forget that the Tower of London is above all a fortress, palatial in size but built with defence very much in mind. Moreover, the most important phases of its construction can still easily be identified by the visitor.

The heart of the castle was, and is, the White Tower, a huge, near-rectangular keep erected in the 1080s by William the Conqueror. Lodged in the south-east corner of London's old Roman walls, and visible from afar in its coat of whitewash (hence its name), the White Tower was intended to protect and also to overawe the city. Its size made it possible for William and his successors to maintain a truly royal state – behind a set of walls up to 15 ft (4·5 m) thick at the base. Despite subsequent building, the general character of the Tower was determined by England's greatest fortress-maker, Edward I. Between 1275 and 1285 he transformed the Tower of London into a concentric castle, surrounding the keep with two rings of curtain walls defended by interval towers. A wide moat was dug, originally filled with water and running along all four sides of the castle. It was linked to the river via a wharf (hence prisoners could be brought to the Tower by boat, entering through 'Traitors' Gate'), extending to the south-west to protect the barbican; the main entrance to the Tower still lies across the moat at this point, but the barbican, or Lion Tower, has vanished, as have the royal apartments of the inner bailey (replaced by barracks and other post-medieval buildings), obscuring the fact that down to the 17th century the Tower rivalled WINDSOR CASTLE (Berkshire) as a palatial fortress or fortified palace.

On the north bank of the River Thames,
east of the City (map page 61)

◆

UPNOR CASTLE   KENT

A distinctive, unusual sight with its great platform thrusting out into the waters of the Medway, Upnor was one of the last fighting castles built in England. It is really an Elizabethan artillery fort, constructed between 1559 and 1567 to protect the ships laid up at the new Chatham dockyards on the opposite (south) bank. The architect was Sir Richard Lee, the military engineer now remembered for his work on the celebrated fortifications of Berwick-upon-Tweed. He put up the rectangular main block of the castle, the two small towers that flanked it, and the Water Bastion, a triangular gun platform on which ordnance could be placed to rake hostile shipping.

In 1599–1601 the castle was greatly strengthened. The towers were enlarged; walls were built out from them on three sides (one with a gatehouse) to form a courtyard, protecting the guns from a rear attack by enemy landing parties; and a parapet was put up on the bastion to shield the guns. During the Civil War, Upnor remained safely in the hands of Parliament except for a single day during which Royalists managed to sieze the castle. Afterwards, in 1653, the last significant changes were made, bricks being used as the material of the clumsy rectangular blocks placed above the gatehouse towers, and also to fill in the hitherto backless towers on the river front.

Upnor's active career began and ended on 12–13 June 1667, when a Dutch fleet sailed up the Medway, destroyed much shipping and carried off the *Royal Charles*. According to the famous diarist Samuel Pepys, the Dutch 'made no more of Upnor's shooting than of a fly', although most home opinion blamed lack of ammunition rather than the shortcomings of the castle for its failure to hold off the enemy. The building of new defences on the Thames made Upnor effectively obsolete, and its later career as a storehouse and powder magazine was uneventful.

2 miles (3 km) north-east of Strood, off
the A228 (map page 61)

◆

WARKWORTH CASTLE   NORTHUMBERLAND

One of the chain of great fortresses stretching along the Northumberland coast, Warkworth is smaller but even more picturesque than ALNWICK and BAMBURGH. Its

Continued on page 150

Guided Tour

WARWICK CASTLE
WARWICKSHIRE

There is no castle in Britain to match Warwick's combination of spectacular stonework and lush natural setting, with the River Avon flowing beneath its south face and 18th-century landscaping shaping the lie of the courtyard within the castle as well as the large and lovely grounds outside. William the Conqueror put up the first castle here in 1068, with a motte on the west side of the oblong bailey. But Warwick acquired its essential character during the 14th century, when the Beauchamp earls transformed it into a showpiece, building sumptuous private apartments against the south curtain wall and reversing the defensive emphasis by creating a magnificent new entrance front on the east side.

It is this façade that the visitor sees after entering the castle precincts through the 18th-century stables. At its corners stand Caesar's Tower (left) and Guy's Tower (right), while the middle of the curtain wall is dominated by a tall, twin-towered gatehouse with a barbican thrusting out into the ditch below it. Caesar's Tower is much the taller, although the fact is only apparent from outside, where its massive battered base can be seen rising up from the river; it is also unusual in plan (trilobate), and in the 'crown' effect created by the smaller battlemented tower rising

above and behind the machicolated parapet. Although a stone bridge has replaced its drawbridge, the barbican is still equipped with a portcullis, and attackers who broke through it and managed to dodge the missiles coming through the murder holes above might still find themselves shot down from the little balcony behind them as they attempted to storm the gatehouse. Like the towers, the barbican and gatehouse

BADGE OF MEDIEVAL
EARLS

GRENADIER'S POUCH
c. 1710

OLIVER CROMWELL'S
DEATH MASK

A fine view of Warwick Castle, with the River Avon in the foreground

plasterwork ceiling of the Blue Boudoir. Close to the exit lies the 14th-century Watergate Tower, now fitted out as an early 17th-century bachelor's quarters, since Sir Fulke Greville, who bought Warwick Castle from James I, lodged here while having the rest of the buildings restored at huge expense.

The Bear and Clarence Towers, on the north curtain, are all that remains of a large fortress projected but never completed by Richard III (1483–5) of evil repute. An entrance in Clarence Tower leads up to a wall-walk and an arduous one-way trip along to Caesar's Tower; an unusual feature between Clarence and Guy's Tower is the 'crow's nest', a small balcony from which the defenders could cover the ground in front of the wall. Separately entered, the basement of Caesar's Tower is a dungeon, said to have held French prisoners after Poitiers (1356), and certainly used during the 17th-century Civil War. The 'Armoury' next door was a late 17th-century brew-house and wash-house.

Madame Tussaud's of London bought Warwick Castle in 1978, and the 19th-century private apartments provide a suitably atmospheric setting for waxwork notables in an accurately re-created 'Royal Weekend Party, 1898'.

Through a gateway in the north curtain lies the old motte, dense with flowering bushes. There are fine long views from the top and, beyond, a delightful variety of parkland pleasures.

In the town, 10 miles (16 km) south-west of Coventry, on the A46 (map page 61)

afforded useful extra accommodation, maximized by careful arrangements and cutting into the thickness of the wall. One neat, intimate suite of rooms is on view, including a small hall – really a sitting room – two chambers, a wash- or store-room, and two privies.

Across the courtyard, reached through the mainly 18th-century chapel, stands the great hall, the principal communal gathering place and the largest room in the castle at 62 × 45 ft (19 × 14 m); unfortunately the fire of 1871 destroyed most of its medieval features. Portraits of historical interest are a feature of the hall and the mainly 17th- and 18th-century state apartments, along with the extraordinary

Warkworth Castle, acquired by the Percys in 1332

Continued from page 147

site is superb, both visually and militarily: it stands on a hill directly above Warkworth village, tucked into a loop in the River Coquet that protects it on three sides. Most unusually, a tower stands on the medieval bridge across the Coquet, guarding the approach to the village and castle.

There were fortifications at Warkworth in Saxon times, and the first castle was put up in the 12th century. But Warkworth is associated above all with the Percy family, who acquired it from Edward III in 1332; it grew in splendour as their power spread through the North, and it was Henry Percy, created Earl of Northumberland in 1377, who erected Warkworth's famous keep or tower house. From most distances and points of view this remarkably designed building, standing high on its mound, commands attention, tempting the visitor to neglect the gatehouse, towers and abundant domestic and ecclesiastical remains. The keep consists of a great square tower with four smaller towers projecting from it, one in the middle of each side; each of the 12 salient points so created is boldly chamfered, giving the building its distinctive multi-faceted appearance. There was ample space inside for a hall, a solar, bedchambers and all the services and comforts a great 14th-century lord expected – all conveniently arranged within the confines of a reputedly impregnable fortress.

However, when the Percys, having put Henry IV on the throne, attempted to unseat him, he marched on Warkworth in 1405 with a train of artillery that quickly compelled the castle to surrender. The family was eventually allowed to repossess it, but the castle declined as their feudal power ebbed. In the 17th century it was twice besieged, slighted and quarried for building materials. Interest in Warkworth only reawakened in the romantically-minded 19th century, when Anthony Salvin restored the keep and brought it up to Victorian standards of gracious living.

**8 miles (13 km) south-east of Alnwick,
on the A1068 (map page 62)**

WHITE CASTLE GWENT

A formidable-looking ruin in open country, White Castle is a good example of a castle adapted, rather than specially built, to incorporate the latest advances in military technology. With Grosmont and Skenfrith, both about $6\frac{1}{2}$ miles (10 km) away, it makes up 'The Three Castles', a triangle of border fortresses designed to control major routes between England and South Wales. White Castle – so-called from the coat of white plaster it once wore – is the best preserved of the three, but it is easy and very worthwhile to visit all three in a single day.

The original timber castle may have been put up by William Fitz Osbern, Earl of Hereford, who directed the Normans' immediate post-Conquest drive against the Welsh in this area; but the certain history of White Castle began in the 12th century, when a square keep and surrounding curtain wall, both of stone, were erected on the site.

In the 1260s or 1270s these defences were modernized, possibly by Prince Edward, later King Edward I and conqueror of Wales. The keep was demolished but the old curtain wall was simply strengthened by the addition of four round towers and a typically powerful twin-towered gatehouse. As part of the same operation, a stone wall with towers was built around the outer bailey or ward to the north; this created a 'safe' area large enough to house an English army, which suggests that White Castle may have been intended to serve as a forward base for an invasion of Wales. Both outer and inner wards are further protected by moats, and the inner ward is sheltered to the south by a crescent-shaped island formerly equipped with outer defences. The accommodation at White Castle seems never to have been luxurious, and by the 16th century, when its military role was unmistakably obsolete, it had already become a ruin.

9 miles (14.5 km) north-east of
Abergavenny, off the B4521 (map page 60)

The royal residence of Windsor Castle

WINDSOR CASTLE BERKSHIRE

Windsor Castle is unique, for it is the largest of all castles (over 13 acres in extent) and has served as a royal residence for over 900 years. It was begun soon after the Conquest by William I and may have been built of stone from the first, since the motte was a high mound of natural chalk, quite strong enough to bear the weight of masonry. Windsor had a shell keep and was already a favourite royal residence under Henry I, but it was Henry II who gave the castle its basic form in the 1170s, building a new shell keep and enclosing the long baileys to the east and west with curtain walls guarded by rectangular interval towers.

Windsor was damaged during the troubles of King John's reign, and rebuilding by his son Henry III (1216–72) included the curtain wall of the lower (west) bailey or ward, on which the towers were rounded in accordance with the latest military thinking. In the 14th century Windsor's exceptional status began to appear, for Edward III was born there and built lavishly inside the keep and around the upper bailey, indulging to the full his passion for chivalric display (notably in the great Hall of St George) and making Windsor Castle the centre of his Order – and cult – of the Garter.

The dominant building in the lower bailey, St George's Chapel, is a masterpiece in the Perpendicular style, begun in 1475 and completed by the Tudors. The most substantial contributions had now been made, but the castle was subject to almost continual modifications. Charles II embellished it, but the greatest volume of work was done in the 19th century, notably by Sir Jeffry Wyatville, who in 1824–6 heightened the keep and reorganized the royal apartments in the upper bailey. With its wealth of exhibitions, furnishings and collections (not to mention Queen Mary's famous dolls' house), Windsor is best visited when the monarch is not in residence and the royal apartments are consequently open to the public.

**On the east side of the town, on the
B3022 (map page 61)**

Glossary of Terms

adulterine describes a castle built without a royal licence

apse rounded end of a building, usually containing its chancel or chapel

arcading row of arches, often 'blind'; that is, appearing only as a low-relief pattern on an otherwise unbroken wall surface

ashlar smooth-faced, squared-off blocks of stone

bailey defended castle enclosure or courtyard

ballista siege weapon resembling a giant crossbow

balustrade row of pillars supporting a parapet

barbican passage or courtyard through which a besieger had to pass to reach the castle gatehouse

bartizan cone-capped projecting turret, characteristic of Scottish castle architecture

bastion gun platform projecting from an angle of the walls of a fortification, exposing attackers on either side to flanking fire

battered describes a wall reinforced so that it slopes outwards towards the base

battery emplacement with a number of artillery pieces

battlements parapet area of a castle wall, usually equipped with crenellations and embrasures

belfry siege tower, built by the besiegers, which could be wheeled up to the castle walls; the attackers then attempted to storm the parapet, crossing on to it by a drawbridge from the top of the belfry

broch round drystone tower, characteristic of the north and west of Scotland from the 1st century BC

burh Saxon fortified town

buttery originally the 'bottlery' where liquors were stored

buttress mass of projecting masonry, functioning as a support for a wall

castellan officer or official in charge of a castle, which he holds for his lord

cat (*see penthouse*)

concentric castle castle with two more or less parallel sets of walls

constable (*see castellan*)

corbel projecting stone block, functioning as a bracket for beams etc

counter-castle structure built close to a besieged castle in order to blockade it or protect the attackers

countermine tunnel dug by the defenders during a siege, intended to break in on, and destroy, a tunnel dug by the besiegers

courtyard castle more or less rectangular castle with walls and towers built round a courtyard and ranges of buildings against the sides; characteristic of the late Middle Ages

crenellation the arrangement of battlements into a line of alternating solids (merlons), offering cover, and voids (crenels)

cross-wall strong, vertical internal wall dividing a keep from top to bottom

cupola a (usually small) dome

curtain non-load-bearing castle wall, often linking towers

ditch dry equivalent to a moat

donjon another term for a keep

drum very large, wide, round tower, usually squat

embrasure a space between two upright merlons on the battlements; or a space cut through a wall, and usually splayed on the inside, so that the defenders could fire on the enemy

enceinte 'girdle' or 'outline'; a castle of enceinte is one defended only by walls and mural towers, that is, with no separate keep

escalade attempting to storm a castle by mounting the walls with ladders

fan vaulting ceiling or roof of complex construction, creating a highly decorative multi-conical effect

fief land held by a noble or knight as the vassal of a lord

forebuilding a structure built against a tower or keep, housing the stairway to the entrance at first-floor level

garderobes alternative term for latrines or lavatories

gargoyle water spout or parapet carved into a grotesque figure

grotto an artificial cavern, arranged with an eye to decorative effect

gunport aperture in a castle wall through which a gun could be fired

half-timbered describes a building of which the framework consists of timber beams, the other parts of the walls being filled with plaster etc

hall keep (*see keep*)

herringbone pattern created by the alternating diagonals in which courses of stones are set; characteristic of early Norman masonry

hillfort type of massive earthwork defence system created by the Celts in the pre-Roman period

honour substantial land-holding, possessed by a great lord

keep main stone building in a castle, characterized by thick walls and arrangements enabling it to be self-sufficient during a siege. When the visual emphasis of the building is vertical, it is a tower keep; when horizontal, a hall keep

loopholes slits in a wall, also known simply as loops, through which a defender could fire

machicolations galleries projecting from a castle exterior; missiles could be dropped on the enemy through holes in their bases

mangonel siege weapon of catapult type

Marcher describes the lords of the Marches, or border lands, close to Wales and Scotland; because of their hazardous location they were often allowed exceptional power and independence

merlons (*see crenellation*)

moat originally the same word as 'motte', 'moat' came to be applied to the ditch dug around the base of the mound. It is still sometimes employed to describe any castle ditch, but everyday language usefully distinguishes between the water-filled moat and the dry ditch

motte the mound on which many medieval British castles were built

mullion a vertical bar dividing a window or opening into two

mural to do with walls; mural towers are towers linked by or incorporated in walls, as opposed to freestanding towers

murder hole opening in a ceiling, through which missiles etc could be thrown down upon attackers

ogee a type of arch; seen in section, the 'onion' top is formed by slightly concave outlines meeting at a pronounced point

ordnance artillery

outworks defensive works lying beyond the main castle area

palisade a timber fence, usually based on a line of stakes

pantry originally the place in a medieval castle or house where bread (French, *pain*) was stored

parapet the battlements wall shielding the castle wall-walk

peel tower (*see pele tower*)

pele tower small, usually very plain keep, built in very large numbers close to the Anglo-Scottish border during the troubled late Middle Ages

penthouse shed or roof used as cover by besiegers attempting to breach a gate or wall; also known as a cat

pilaster a flattened column projecting shallowly from a wall and forming strip-like decoration in low relief

portcullis heavy grid, raised and lowered by windlass, used to reinforce a castle gate

postern small castle entrance/exit, additional to the main gateway(s); also known as a sallyport

putlog holes square holes in a stone surface into which the ends of wooden beams were fitted; the timber has rotted, but in many medieval castles the putlog holes remain

ringwork defensive arrangement consisting of a ditch dug all round a camp or settlement; the earth removed is heaped up on the inner side of the ditch to create high ramparts, which may be surmounted by a palisade

sallyport (*see postern*)

sham castle edifice that looks like a castle, but whose apparently military features are in fact only ornamental

shell keep not really a keep at all, this consists of a wall, with or without towers, built around the top of a motte. In a few instances the 'shell' is built up from the base of the motte

slight to disable a castle, damaging it badly enough to make it indefensible

solar living room on an upper floor of a castle or house

stucco plasterwork

tenants-in-chief the principal vassals of the king, holding lands directly from him; the great nobles

tower house a term used as an alternative to keep, especially where the tower house is relatively small. Much used of Scottish keeps

trébuchet siege weapon, essentially a large sling worked by counterweights

turret small tower

vassal man who has done homage to a lord in return for protection, land etc

wall-walk the walkway behind a castle parapet, enabling the garrison to patrol, or fight from, the stretch of wall between two towers

ward castle enclosure; sometimes used in preference to 'bailey', especially of castles built after the mid 13th century

yett hinged iron grille used to reinforce a tower-house gate in Scotland and northern England

Index

Acknowledgements

———◆———

The photographs in *Castles* were supplied by the photographers and agencies listed below:

AA Photolibrary pp. 15, 44, 50, 72, 87, 99, 100–1, 105, 108, 115, 117, 125, 128–9, 130, 133, 135, 138, 141, 144
Jeffrey Beazley pp. 30, 33, 91
John Bethell pp. 2, 6, 8, 12, 18, 20, 24–5 (and front cover), 27, 38, 40–1, 47, 52, 55, 57, 71, 75, 78–9, 80, 83, 94, 110, 112, 120, 123
Ian Booth p. 148–9
Impact Photos/Tony Page p. 67
Marianne Majerus p. 35
National Trust Photographic Library/Derry Robinson p.64
The line drawings are by Lyn Cawley, and the castle illustrations in the gazetteer are by Sheilagh Noble.
The maps on pp. 60–3 were drawn by John Gilkes.